DECORATING FOR THE
HOLIDAYS

Christmas with Martha Stewart Living

DECORATING FOR THE
HOLIDAYS

Clarkson Potter/Publishers
New York

Originally published in book form by
Martha Stewart Living Omnimedia LLC
in 1998.
Published simultaneously by Clarkson N.
Potter, Inc., Oxmoor House, Inc., and
Leisure Arts.

A portion of this work was previously
published in MARTHA STEWART LIVING.

Published by Clarkson N. Potter, Inc.,
201 East 50th Street, New York,
NY 10022.
Member of the Crown Publishing Group.
Random House, Inc. New York, Toronto,
London, Sydney, Auckland
http://www.randomhouse.com
Clarkson N. Potter, Potter, and colophon
are trademarks of Clarkson N. Potter, Inc.

Printed in the United States of America.

Library of Congress
Cataloging-in-Publication Data
Stewart, Martha
Decorating for the Holidays: Christmas
with Martha Stewart Living: The Best of
Martha Stewart Living.
p. cm.
1. Christmas decorations. 2. Handicraft.
I. Martha Stewart Living.
TT900.C4D426 1998 745.594'.12—dc21
98-20389
ISBN 0-609-80336-0 (alk. paper)

10 9 8 7 6 5 4 3 2 1
First Edition

Produced by Eric A. Pike
Text by Terry Trucco
Art Director: Linda Kocur
Senior Editor: Bruce Shostak
Copy Editor: Annie Block

CONTENTS

INTRODUCTION

It may be hard to believe, my having worked on so many books and articles pertaining to the winter holidays, but I still look forward to celebrating Christmas. Every year, I am entranced by the beauty of the season, I am enamored of new and lovely ways to decorate a tree or a doorway or a window, and I am enlivened anew each time I see an old-fashioned gingerbread cookie or a crèche or a house bedecked with twinkling lights. ✳ The Christmas season for me is still about the birth of Christ, the adoration of the Magi, and the manger in Bethlehem. But it is also about other festivals celebrated late in the month of December, including Hanukkah and Kwanza, as well as New Year's Eve and Day. I have become more and more curious about how these holidays are observed and about the family traditions that are intertwined with each holiday's religious and cultural customs. ✳ This book is meant to help you glorify and beautify your home, inside and outside, for the holidays. It is also a sourcebook for ideas that will help you entertain and prepare gifts and adornments for your own holiday celebrations. Keeping family traditions alive and cherished is one of the most wonderful things you can do for your family. A simple gesture, a handmade ornament, a special Christmas confection—these are the things that cause our spirits to soar and our hearts to burst with pleasure during the festive season. ✳ Many people worked on this volume, and many others contributed ideas and inspiration for the extraordinarily fine assortment of craft and decorating projects and recipes, and I am proud to be a part of this team. All of us at Martha Stewart Living wish you and your families a very merry Christmas and a happy New Year this year and for many years to come.

Martha Stewart

part 1

DECK THE HALLS

NOW IS THE TIME
TO EMBRACE WINTER. CAPTURE
THE WANING DAYLIGHT
WITH FLICKERING CANDLES
AND STRINGS OF
WINKING LIGHTS.
INVITE NATURE'S
GREENERY TO BE A GUEST
IN EVERY ROOM,
JUST WHEN YOU BEGIN TO MISS
THE OUTDOORS MOST.
LET YOUR HOUSE SMILE
AT ALL WHO PASS,
OR PERHAPS
LET A SNOWMAN
DO THE JOB.

SNOWMEN

*Winter's unofficial mascots bring light,
whimsy, and cheer to the season
of short days and icy nights*

Nothing animates a blanketed winter landscape, brightens a biting-cold day, or thaws a frosty disposition quite like a snowman. Whether gazing from a hilltop or guarding the front yard, snowmen announce that winter is here—and all is well. While their presence as symbols of the Christmas season may date back only to the early part of the nineteenth century, the urge to shape snow into life-size figures probably stretches back farther, to the first time humans saw snow. Like clay or cookie dough, snow practically demands to be shaped. Who can resist? So bundle up and get rolling. ✳ As snowmen go, there is nothing wrong with the classic three-baller, but snow is such a versatile medium you can easily coax it into more unexpected shapes. The most elaborate snow creatures require wooden skeletons for support, but these structures needn't be fancy—a few scraps of wood screwed or nailed together will usually do the trick. ✳ The best time to build a snowman is when the thermometer hovers at thirty-four degrees, and the snow is neither powder nor slush. You can simulate these conditions on colder days by spritzing warm water on the snow until it feels light and moist and packs well. After that, dress up your snowman with anything from your house or yard: vegetables and cookies, berries and pinecones, tinsel and tinfoil. A snowman, after all, will thrive wearing just about anything, except a suntan.

CHRISTMAS HELPERS
With her dog, our snow girl (opposite) trims a tree with silver-glass ornaments and snowballs hung from wire. She wears tinsel; his collar is tinfoil. Our snow bear (previous pages, left), wearing a pine-sprig vest and shorts made out of pinecones, untangles a string of tiny lights to decorate a pine tree. Leading a lone reindeer across a frozen lake, a skinny Santa (previous page) pulls a sleigh of snowy parcels.

SCULPTING IN SNOW

modern-day visions of old-fashioned friends

SNOW BEAR Build a six-foot wooden skeleton to support the bear from two-by-twos using an electric drill equipped with a screwdriver bit. Screw skeleton to a two-foot-by-two-foot plywood base, and bury the base in the snow to keep the bear from toppling under his own weight. Dampen the wood using a spray bottle filled with warm water so the snow sticks. Pack snow around the wood; spritz each layer with warm water so it freezes. Once you have built a sufficient base of snow to flesh out the bear, leave the sculpture to freeze overnight. The next day, add the final coat, and sculpt the bear's generous proportions more precisely. Add the bear's vest by poking sprigs of pine into the snow. To create his lederhosen, wire pinecones to wooden dowels (below left), and insert them into the snow. An old black fedora with a pine-sprig feather sits on his head; his eyes and nose are made of dried prunes. Although carrots and coal are the classic choices for a snowman's features, you can use almost anything you like, especially biodegradables that will blend into the ground as gracefully as your snowman.

SKINNY SANTA Using an electric drill equipped with a screwdriver bit, build wooden skeletons for Santa and his reindeer out of two-by-fours and two-by-twos. Affix each skeleton to its own plywood platform for stability. To make the antlers, wire bare branches to the reindeer's head before packing the wood frame with snow (above left). Apply the first coat of snow; use a spray bottle filled with warm water to dampen the wood so the snow sticks to it, and to moisten the snow so it packs firmly. Leave this coat of snow to freeze overnight; it will provide a solid underpinning for the shapes. The next day, add the second layer of snow (above right), shaping it with your hands and small garden tools, spritzing as you go to keep the snow solid. The Santa is outfitted with black gloves, a red elf's hat, and silver balls as buttons. The reindeer gets Oreo eyes, a collar of millinery berries, a stocking cap, and ornaments to dangle from his antlers. Make the presents on the sled by packing snow in plastic containers, popping them out, then decorating them with berries and pine sprigs.

SNOW GIRL Begin by making four-foot stick figures of one-by-twos screwed to plywood bases using an electric drill fitted with a screwdriver bit. Pack snow around wood, and spritz each layer with water so it freezes. Edge the girl's dress with tinsel, securing it in place with hairpins; fashion the dog's collar and trim out of folded tinfoil. To make snowball ornaments that hang on the tree, use a plastic snowball maker (below right): Attach a loop of wire to a twig, embed it in the snow, and press a snowball into place around it so loop emerges.

SNOWBALL CLOWN *Dressed in white, a mischievous cousin of the familiar three-ball Frosty balances atop a snowdrift pedestal dotted with red votives. The necklaces that ring his body are created with a snowball maker, and are frozen in place with spritzes of water. The clown's conical hat is made from snow molded in a funnel. He has pinecone eyes and a turnip nose.*

SNOW PRINCESS *Like their summer relative the sand castle, snow creatures can be made in any style, shape, or size you wish. Part of the fun is creating snowmen that find themselves in amusing situations or settings, and exude personality. Our snow princess presides over a court of willow branches—the same elements that make up her arms and decorate the hem of her generous skirt. To create her gown, pack snow into a five-foot trumpet shape, and sculpt her bodice at the top; add a snowball for her head. Adorn the gown with pinecones and rosettes (opposite, bottom center). Make each rosette on a disc of cardboard through which you've inserted a long nail; hot-glue pinecones and almonds to the disc, and push the nail into the snow. Dress up her waist and neckline with juniper sprigs, and crown her with a large pinecone.*

FRONT
DOORS

*Celebrating begins at your doorstep
with wreaths and swags made
from winter's harvest*

With only gray skies surrounding it, a house in early winter can look stark. But hang a wreath or a swag on the front door, and your house will spring to life. Cuttings of evergreen are sweet compensation for the leaves that are missing from most of the trees, and the tart hues of winter berries are reminders that nature has not forgotten about color, even though the garden is no longer in bloom. Add wide ribbons and twinkling lights, and holiday spirit brims over. ✳ The Victorians, who never willingly left a surface unadorned, are sometimes credited with the custom of hanging Christmas wreaths on front doors. In more recent years, front-door displays have taken many forms, from flashy tinsel wreaths with silver-metallic bows to electric-light garlands that spell out "Season's Greetings." The most eloquent outdoor ornaments, however, are usually simple and natural, made from the hearty fruit and greenery that flourish while almost all of the landscape hibernates. ✳ Winter's harvest abounds with unexpected textures and shapes, like spiky pinecones and smooth little eucalyptus seeds. And the palette is more than the red and green we expect. We do get those colors, of course, in abundance: scarlet cranberries, blood-red rose hips, crimson Pyracantha, and a cavalcade of greenery—silver-green eucalyptus, blue-green cedar, deep-green boxwood, and the astonishing chartreuse and olive-green of

CRANBERRY ROPES
Wrapped on a large wreath of contrasting greens and strung with crimson ribbon through two small wreaths, strands of cranberries (opposite) gleam like rubies. A luxuriant rondel in blues and greens (previous pages, left) is made of bunches of purple privet berries mixed with holly and eucalyptus leaves. A boxwood ball strung with little white lights (previous pages, right) glows in a doorway.

the intriguingly named golden hinoki false cypress. But there is also the tangy purple of privet berries, the spongy gold of kumquats, and the yellow pods and wild-red centers of bittersweet. ✳ To make decorations for your front door, you may find all the raw materials you need growing in your own yard or garden, but if you don't, visit

garden centers, florists, Christmas-tree lots, even greengrocers. If the greenery you have chosen feels sappy or prickly, be sure to wear work gloves. And remember that although there is nothing wrong with a big spray of holly tied with a red bow, embellishing the traditional recipes can yield lovely results. We finished a large wreath with crisscrossed strings of

KUMQUAT SWIRLS *To set a festive mood on a portico (opposite), bay-laurel garlands are wrapped with strings of kumquats, then twisted around the columns. The kumquats are strung end to end on 24-gauge floral wire; kumquats and lemons are also wired into the blue-spruce spray on the door. Pillar candles, anchored by kumquats in large canning jars, illuminate the steps and walkway (left) and won't blow out easily. Attach some floral adhesive to the bottom of each candle to secure it in the jar.*

cranberries instead of a bow, and turned a classic boxwood ball, constructed on three single-wire wreath forms, into a unique outdoor chandelier by adding a string of white lights and hanging it from a chain of little pinecones. Once you have learned how to cut and wire greenery, our outdoor ornaments are easy to construct and make enjoyable projects for brisk winter days, especially when you are working with fragrant greens. If you select cuttings that are as fresh as possible, and the weather stays cold, your outdoor displays should last for weeks, spreading holiday cheer throughout the season.

MAKING WIRED DOOR ORNAMENTS

boxwood lantern, cranberry-laced wreath, and "Noel" greeting

BOXWOOD LANTERN The evergreen-and-pinecone globe on page 19 can be suspended from a porch ceiling or hung in a foyer in place of a chandelier. To make it, you will need three 12" single-wire wreath forms; 26-gauge or lighter floral wire; boxwood; small pinecones 1" to 1½" long; 75-bulb strand of white outdoor lights; and a cup hook. Boxwood, a durable green, comes in two strains: American boxwood has long, thin leaves; English boxwood has rounder, fuller leaves. English boxwood is more expensive than American boxwood, but you'll need to use less because it's thicker. 1. Position the wreath forms as shown, so the six spokes fan out evenly. Wire them together tightly at the top and bottom, lashing the wire among all the spokes; once secure, snip the wire. If possible, make this a two-person job: One holds the wreath forms steady; the other wires them together. 2. At one of the poles, secure the end of the floral wire to one of the frames. Attach a small bundle of boxwood tips, wrapping it in place with floral wire. Work your way down the spoke, adding boxwood, until you reach the other intersection; tie off the wire. Repeat on remaining five spokes until the entire frame is covered. When finished, fluff the boxwood leaves with your fingers to hide any wire that remains exposed. To illuminate the globe, wrap the outdoor lights around spokes. You can start wrapping at any point of the ball, but make sure the unlit portion of the cord, with the plug at its end, winds up extending like a tail from top of ball. Wrap the cord 2 to 3 times around the top, and wrap floral wire a few times around cord and ball to keep them attached. Wrap lights securely, but not too tightly; ruffle boxwood leaves to cover the electrical wire. 3. Cover exposed cord with the small pinecones. On floral wire, attach a pinecone every 1½" by wrapping wire around the top of the pinecone. Beginning at the ball, wind this pinecone garland around and around the electrical cord; add more pinecones as needed. 4. Wrap pinecones almost flush with the plug. To hang the ball, screw a cup hook into the ceiling, and hook the end of the cord through, letting the plug serve as an anchor. Add extra boxwood at the top to cover the hook and wires. Use an outdoor-grade extension cord to reach the nearest outlet. To avoid electrical hazards, always use caution with outdoor lights.

CRANBERRY-LACED WREATH The large, cranberry-wrapped wreath looks as handsome on a window or wall as it does on a front door. The two small wreaths and strands of ribbon and cranberries that frame it on page 20 can also be used to decorate an interior window or mirror. To make entire arrangement, you'll need a 20" tubular straw-wreath form; two 6" single-wire wreath forms; floral pins; 24-gauge floral wire; golden hinoki false cypress; cranberries; and 4"-wide ribbon. We chose this greenery because the dark cranberries stand out against its varied hues of green; light-colored fancy cedar can also be used. 1. To make large wreath, place straw-wreath form on a table, and, using floral pins, attach sprigs of greenery all the way around. Vary the wreath's color by alternating light, medium, and dark greens. 2. To make cranberry strands: First twist one end of a length of floral wire into a knot. String cranberries, one by one, onto wire, piercing each berry from end to end. Finish the strand with another knot, to keep berries on wire. 3. To

decorate the wreath, lay strands of berries on the wreath to plot a crisscross pattern; use floral pins to indicate where the strands intersect. Be sure the ends of the strands fall on the back of the wreath. When you are pleased with the pattern, anchor the cranberry strands with floral pins. Draping the cranberry strands can be difficult so, if possible, have someone help you: One person holds the wreath and the other weaves the strands. To recreate the doorway decorations on page 20, make two wreaths using 6" wire-wreath forms, floral wire, and sprigs of golden hinoki false cypress (follow the techniques described in step 2 for the Boxwood Lantern). Hang each wreath from nails placed above opposite sides of the door. Thread two cranberry strands and a long length of satin ribbon through the two wreaths. The ribbon and cranberry strands should swoop gracefully above the door. When the ribbon and cranberry strands are positioned correctly, cut the ribbon ends on a diagonal.

"NOEL" GREETING To make the greeting on the following page, you'll need fancy cedar; 14-gauge wire; 26-gauge or lighter floral wire; wire pliers; scissors; stapler; plywood work surface; paper; and marker. Write your greeting on a piece of paper, or use a printed greeting, and enlarge it on a photocopier to the size you want.

Or you can write your holiday message to scale with a marker. Attach the paper to a piece of plywood or an old table that can be used as a work surface. To create a metal form for the greeting, use 14-gauge wire from a spool. 1. Bend the wire to start a letter, stapling down the wire at the turn. 2. Bend next segment after you've stapled the turn—you'll find it is easier. 3. To secure wires wherever they cross, as they do in this L, twist the floral wire around itself. When the wire form is complete, remove the staples with pliers. 4. Using floral wire, attach fancy cedar to the wire form, as described in step 2 for the Boxwood Lantern. Be sure to wire the greens so letters will be legible. Snip off any scraggly ends for a neat appearance.

CEDAR GREETING *All garlands convey holiday cheer, but a handwritten garland is an exuberant way to make certain no one misses the point. Our "Noel" greeting is made by attaching fancy cedar to a homemade heavy-wire form. The script letters allow the word to flow in an unbroken line. So the garland will be legible, be sure the greenery wrapped around the wire is not too bushy.*

TRIO OF WREATHS *Who said a door should have only one wreath? These wreaths are made from eucalyptus and juniper leaves and are studded with their respective seeds and berries. The large wreath is wired on a 16" wire-wreath form, while the two smaller companions are on 10" forms. The wide silver ribbon is looped over the top of the door and secured with thumbtacks.*

FIVE-WREATH SWAG *Our merry chain of miniature wreaths on a length of taffeta ribbon shows that wreaths don't need to hang on the door at all. First, wire sprigs of boxwood to five 6" single-wire wreath forms. Using a very wide ribbon, which will make plump knots and billow between the wreaths, tie each wreath along the ribbon in a single knot. To hang the garland, insert a nail or hook at each side of the doorway; then, using floral wire, secure the wreaths at the ends of the swags to the nails or hooks. If the weight of the middle wreaths causes the garland to sag, you may need to support the wreaths with small tacks.*

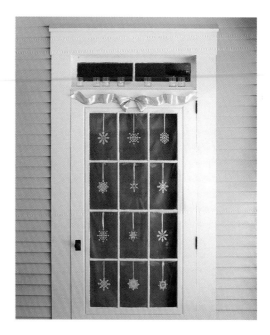

SNOWFLAKE DOOR *Suspended by narrow silver ribbons tacked to each muntin, a collection of glittered snowflake ornaments sparkles in the sunlight, elegantly displayed in a door's window panes. Above the door, antique silver ribbon is tied into a bow; its undulating streamers are held in place by floral adhesive. Votive candles set along the transom add more sparkle at nightfall.*

LIGHTED PINE FESTOONS *Two lines of illuminated white-pine garlands, reminiscent of old-fashioned bunting, create a scalloped edge beneath a house's eaves (opposite). The bottom swag is wrapped with strands of large bulbs, while the top swag is lit by minilights. In the yard is a tepee Christmas tree, constructed from five tree branches and lengths of white-pine garland.*

MAGNOLIA BANISTER *Such lavish magnolia-leaf garlands can be expensive, but they will be worth it for that special holiday party. The white lights show off the brown and green sides of the magnolia leaves and gently illuminate the porch at dusk. First, wrap strings of lights loosely around the garland. Before hanging, lay the garlands on the floor to plot out the pattern. Then attach them to the banister one at a time with 26-gauge floral wire or clear heavy-duty monofilament. We put these outdoor lights on a dimmer, for even more mood.*

GARLANDS &
BLOSSOMS

Welcome nature indoors
with evergreen boughs
and the prettiest blooms

Evergreens are so natural and neutral, you can drape great swags of them anywhere—over mirrors, around banisters, from picture rails. They are not meant to be permanent, but that is part of their charm. Without nature's prettiest and lushest offerings—evergreens for garlands and wreaths, and fresh blooms for bouquets—a house is not quite dressed for the holidays. ✳ Garlands are like gift-wrapping for your rooms. Making them is an easy two-step process. First use wire and twine to construct a narrow length of thin, pliable branches called a base garland. Then you completely cover it with decorative greens. We made some of our garlands entirely with one type of green, like fragrant bay leaf or feathery white pine. Evergreens can also be combined to create beguiling textures and contrasts; when woven through a swag of blue spruce, sprigs of seeded and weeping eucalypti shimmer like tendrils of silver lace. You can make garlands as slim or as full as you like. They can swell at the middle and taper toward the ends, like our neoclassical boxwood swags. The beauty of evergreens lies in the length, color, and complexity of their needles or leaves, so most call for little embellishment other than ribbons. ✳ Your own property may contain the boughs you need. Cutting greenery from your own trees and shrubs is not just economical, it can also be good for them. Blue atlas cedar, for example, is by nature

AMARYLLIS BOUQUETS
At Christmas, display flowers and greenery in unexpected ways. Use cut amaryllis in big bunches (opposite); these sit below an antique barometer adorned with sprigs of greens and berries. Treat garlands, like these tapering swags of boxwood (previous pages, left) like neoclassical architectural details. Or use a nontraditional vase, like an English transfer-ware soup tureen (previous page), to hold a radiant bouquet of roses, ranunculus, tulips, and striated carnations.

a little sparse, and pruning the tips helps it grow back fuller. Evergreens that have needles should not be heavily pruned—cut a pine-tree branch to the trunk, and it will never grow back—but you can safely trim the smaller offshoots down to the main branch, shaping the tree as you go. ✳ The evergreens in this chapter will either dry beautifully or stay lush and supple for about three weeks, long enough to get through the holidays. And they last even longer if they are used outdoors or set in water— greenery makes wonderful arrangements. ✳ Flowers will not last as long as evergreens, but they are more welcome than ever. On a winter morning, a bowl of silky tulips can seem like a tiny miracle. Use the season's traditional blooms, or other favorite flowers, in unexpected ways. Cut from their bulbs and arranged in a vase, amaryllis seem even more vibrant and exotic. Paper-whites are endearing planted in individual pots and grouped on a tray atop a small table or mantel. Instead of a favorite vase or urn, employ a pretty household item, like a sugar bowl or coffee pot, then fill it with flowers that show it off.

LOOPED BAY LAUREL
A bay-laurel garland (opposite) adds a bold gesture above a window. Construct the garland from two lengths of greenery: Hang the longer length from a nail at the left side, then loop it on a nail at center. Wire the shorter length to the loop, and hang to the right so the leaves point outward. Filling the window is a stem of fragrant casablanca lilies. Thriving in the light of another window are paper-whites in glazed ceramic pots (left): each flower would make a lovely gift or favor.

To complement the intricate patterns on an English transferware soup tureen, we introduced a handful of striated carnations to a mix of tulips, roses, ranunculus, and magnolia leaves. ✳ When it comes to decking the halls, no one provides better materials than nature.

MISTLETOE GARLAND AND WREATHS *Take the artwork off the walls, and replace it with greenery. Here, two ten-foot mistletoe garlands meet above a center wreath hung from cheerful yellow ribbon; smaller wreaths are suspended over the windows—the room needs no other embellishment. To make these, wire tight, compact clusters of mistletoe over a base garland.*

TRAILING GARLANDS *A garland of golden hinoki false cypress, anchored with green velvet bows, frames a doorway. Although it looks like one continuous garland, it's actually three—one down each side of the door, and a third swagged across the top—because the garlands are too thick to fold into sharp corners. Constructing it in sections also allows you to control the direction of the greenery. If this were one garland, the sprigs would face upward on one side of the door. Wire bunches of this evergreen to three base garlands in lengths that correspond to your doorway, and hang. On the staircase, intertwined garlands of olive and white pine lend a rich mix of texture and color. The silvery olive-branch leaves complement white pine's long needles; let the ends trail to the floor. Finish by twisting a string of cranberries around the garland—we used wooden ones; real cranberries last only several days indoors.*

PICTURE-WIRE GARLAND *You can embellish almost anything in your house with flowers and greenery. In this hallway, an eighteenth-century French gilt mirror appears to be suspended from garlands of fancy cedar and seeded eucalyptus. The mirror is actually hung from behind on a picture hook; the garlands are tucked behind the frame and only seem to support the mirror. On the nineteenth-century French mahogany table, ranunculuses and lily tulips evoke the season as readily as poinsettias or amaryllis. The flowers, their stems snipped short, are massed in a Sheraton-style sugar bowl flanked by Sheraton-style silver candlesticks. To achieve the varied height of the arrangement, gather either flower into small bunches of three or four blooms each, bind each bunch with floral tape, then build bouquet, bunch by bunch.*

IDENTIFYING GREENERY

a glossary of our long-lasting favorites

1. MISTLETOE Dries to a shade of chartreuse in about a week. Mistletoe berries are toxic; many will have fallen from the plant by December, but any that remain should be removed by hand. If you have children or pets, choose another kind of greenery.

2. BLUE ATLAS CEDAR This accent tree, found in many yards, has short, tufting needles that make flexible and durable decorations.

3. BAY LEAF The fragrant, elongated leaves provide a great contrast to the more familiar needles. Bay leaves dry like a dream: The color fades slightly, and the leaves curl gently.

4. WHITE PINE Probably the most common on the East Coast, this greenery is soft, durable, flexible, and inexpensive. Pine produces more pitch than other evergreens, making it very flammable, so be careful with it as it dries.

5. BOXWOOD With its small, dense, shiny leaves, boxwood is versatile for classic garlands and wreaths. Because it grows slowly, it can be expensive.

6. OLIVE This California native, which bears fruit from late July to January, dries with little change to its silver-backed leaves. The more readily available Russian Olive has similar leaves but no olives.

7. GOLDEN HINOKI FALSE CYPRESS Also known as Crippsii—short for Chamaecyparis obtusa 'Crippsii'—this evergreen is excellent for wreaths and garlands, as it dries slowly and holds up well.

8. COLORADO BLUE SPRUCE This stately and elegant evergreen has sharp, stiff needles, so wear heavy work gloves when making decorations with it. Indoors, it will usually start dropping needles in about a week, so use it only for last-minute decorations, or use it to decorate the outside of your home.

9. & 10. SEEDED AND WILLOW EUCALYPTI These eucalyptus trees, as well as other varieties, offer great texture, dimension, and fragrance. They also hold their color well.

11. PRINCESS PINE This delicate and lacy evergreen dries, indoors, in about a week; it lasts longer in water.

LEARNING TO WIRE GREENERY

basic techniques for making wreaths and garlands

MAKING A WREATH Attach 22-gauge floral wire on a paddle to a single-wire wreath form by wrapping end of wire tightly around form two times. Lay a bundle of greenery on form, and wrap wire tightly around stems. Wrap a second time, moving wire down length of greenery. Wrap wire a third time, but now moving backwards; this "backwiring" will strengthen wreath—it's especially useful for controlling bushy greenery. Continue adding greenery (right), overlapping each bundle by half. When finished, secure wire with knot, and cut.

MAKING A GARLAND A garland that is sturdy, flexible, and uniform is made in two parts: The base garland, invisible on the finished product, is a supporting structure of thin, pliable, woody branches (they don't have to be attractive, or even evergreen) tightly wired to twine. The outer garland is made by adding bunches of decorative greenery to the base. You'll need a ball of sturdy twine; 22-gauge floral wire on a paddle; garden clippers; wire cutters; work gloves; branches for garland base (we used Douglas fir, but you can use whatever is available); and branches of decorative greenery. 1. To anchor your garland, use a chair pushed under a table or other work surface. Tie end of ball of twine to chair, leaving a one-foot tail. Secure end of floral wire directly to twine. Extend twine along work surface. 2. Hold a few branches of the base material firmly against twine, and wrap wire around both twine and branches very tightly. Make a second wrap, moving wire several inches down length of branches. Wrap wire around a third time, this time moving back toward chair. This extra step, "backwiring," is what makes entire garland secure and flexible. Continue adding branches, overlapping each addition by more than half and repeating wiring and backwiring. Make base as long as you want the finished garland to be. Cut floral wire, and secure end to twine. Leave a foot of twine at end, and cut. 3. The finished base garland is thin and uniform, ready for embellishment. 4. Add decorative greenery. Go back to chair end, and attach floral wire (for delicate greenery, use thinner wire) to base. On work surface, arrange sprigs of greenery—here we used boxwood—all around and along base, so garland looks uniform. Wire and backwire greenery to base, as described in step two. 5. Finish wiring greenery to the base. Cut floral wire, and secure end around twine. Untie the other end from the chair. Use the uncovered twine for hanging.

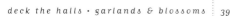

DECORATING WITH SWAGS

blue-spruce and bay-leaf garland, olive garland, and pomegranate festoon

BLUE-SPRUCE AND BAY-LEAF GARLAND A garland hung on a wall can be part of an arrangement of pictures, objects, and furniture you already have in place. The silvery-gray ribbons and tiny silver-glass balls that adorn our garland of Colorado blue spruce and bay leaf (opposite) complement the mercury-glass lamp base and silver tray on the table. To make the garland, construct a base garland, as described on page 39, then wire sprigs of spruce and bay leaves on top. Make the garland in two pieces with all the needles and leaves pointing in the same direction; attach them with floral wire at the left bend, so both sides point downward. If you cannot get the garland to "turn" on a sharp angle, make it in three separate pieces. Wire the silver-glass balls into the garland (left). If you want to give shiny silver balls a matte finish, coat them with a dulling spray (available at crafts stores); let the balls dry before adding them to the garland. Tie ribbons to the corners, and hang the garland from two nails.

OLIVE GARLAND Our olive garland (following page, left) loops around three wreath forms. The garland is meant to be thin and airy, so you don't need to make a base garland. Measure the length that you want garland to be, and add the circumferences of the three wreath forms; cut a piece of twine to this length. Cut 5" sprigs from olive branches, and, using 22-gauge floral wire on a paddle, secure them to twine. Keep adding sprigs along entire length of twine (below left). Lay finished garland on a flat work surface, and arrange it so it lies on top of a single-wire wreath form. Wire garland to form (below right). Add other two wreath forms. At top of each wreath, garland will be thicker; to thin it, remove some leaves. Make three loops of ribbon, and hang garland and wreaths from wall. To shape arcs at ends of garlands, use tacks or straight pins in the wall.

POMEGRANATE FESTOON This delicate and colorful garland (following page, right) is built on a base of thin twine. Use a Dremel rotary tool with a thin bit to drill through dried pomegranates (bottom left), which are available at crafts stores; you'll need six per running yard of garland. Cut a piece of twine a little longer than you want garland to be. Tie a double knot near one end; thread other end through a big craft needle. Send needle through a pomegranate, so it rests against knot. Make a second knot on other side of pomegranate to keep it in place. Make a third knot about 6" along twine. Add another pomegranate; secure with another knot. Keep making knots and adding fruit, 6" apart, along entire length of twine. Fill spaces between pomegranates with bay leaves (bottom right): Cut 6" sprigs, poke ends into hole in pomegranate, and use short pieces of floral wire to secure sprigs to twine. Continue, adding bay leaves between all fruit. The "tassels" at ends are sprigs inserted directly in holes.

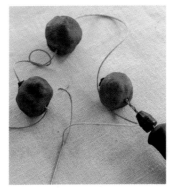

OLIVE GARLAND *Olive's long, delicate leaves are perfect for creating an airy, sinuous garland to replace art or a mirror above a mantel. Although we made our looped garland (above left) from a continuous length of greenery, you can alternatively cover three single-wire wreath forms with greens, and wire them to connecting swags. Deep-green satin ribbon holds the garland and decorates the olive wreath above the fire, where the streamers are held in place with floral adhesive. An assortment of pillar candles, glass ornaments, and merrily wrapped boxes fills the mantel.*

POMEGRANATE FESTOON *Alone or incorporated into a garland, dried pomegranates are nature's version of red ornaments. They're loosely strung with bay leaves to form this light, lacy garland (above right), perfect for draping over a mirror, especially one with in a gilded frame. The garland is made from four separate lengths, which allowed us to point the bay leaves downward on the side swags, like long tassels. Such an informal garland is a suitable companion for the simple antique pine demilune below it. Cut amaryllis in antique-glass vases provide additional strokes of red and green.*

EUCALYPTUS "CURTAINS" *Glamorous swags of weeping and seeded eucalyptus hang like curtains across the tops and down the inner sides of two living-room windows. Wide satin ribbons tied at the corner of each swag add to the swoop. A boxwood ball in a glass compote atop the chest is a substitute for flowers or a tabletop tree. To make the ball, see page 24.*

part 2

TRIM THE TREE

THIS MOMENT
BRINGS CHRISTMAS HOME.
THE TREE, TOWERING
OR TINY, IS UP. TO EVERY BOUGH,
TIE A GLISTENING
BAUBLE OR A HANDMADE
HEIRLOOM BALL
OR A COOKIE FRAGRANT
WITH SPICES.
THEN, LOOK AROUND.
USE YOUR PRETTIEST
ORNAMENTS IN
SUNLIT WINDOWS,
IN A FOOTED SILVER BOWL,
OR AS LITTLE TOKENS
HUNG ON THE KNOB OF
A LOVED ONE'S
DOOR.

FABRICS & TRIMMINGS

dressy or homey, silky or metallic,
they can clothe any tree
or cradle the smallest gifts

Dressing your house in the fabrics of Christmas is as satisfying as wrapping yourself in the sensuous silk scarf or velvet jacket you save for the holidays. Fabric brings richness, color, and depth to any shape it embraces— almost demanding to be touched, whether it is a scratchy wool or a buttery silk. Trims are the finishing touches that shimmer and delight, like icing on cookies. ✳ Fabric has been woven into holiday decorating since Victorian times. Before the Christmas stocking evolved, real socks, often embroidered or trimmed, were hung near chimneys, with high hopes. At the turn of the century, fancifully shaped animals and figures made from snowy cotton batting wrapped on metal frames dangled from countless American Christmas trees. Our voluptuous fabric-covered ball ornaments, which were inspired by similar ornaments made by the Austrian mother of one of Martha's friends, carry on the tradition of draping a tree in fabric. ✳ Fabrics and trims are remarkably versatile materials for craft projects: They can be cut, pinned, sewn, and tied into ornaments as glamorous as our big kissing ball or as simple as our miniature felt stockings for an Advent tree. And although some of our beribboned stockings require that you have strong sewing skills, you can create the sumptuous Christmas-tree balls in luminous fabrics without ever sewing a stitch. ✳ With so many fabrics and trims available,

KISSING BALL *Framed by a garland of cedar and eucalyptus, a ten-inch taffeta ball (opposite) hangs from silver ribbon looped and pinned to the top. Smaller versions of this ball clothe a majestic Christmas tree (previous pages, left), along with metallic ribbon and silver-glass ornaments. To trim our silk and velvet ornaments and stockings, we chose a wide selection of metallic-silver cord, ribbons, rickrack, and other trimmings, as well as tassels, tassel balls, and pearl-head pins (previous pages, right).*

how do you begin to choose? We used dressy fabrics like silk-faced satin, silk taffeta, and velvet for most of our ornaments and stockings, and finished them with a wide selection of metallic-silver ribbons, bullion, rickrack, and twine, all of which take on a soft, nearly golden patina over time. But almost any winter fabrics will do, from

woolly tartans and humble corduroys to an old Christmas tablecloth, too worn to be used for dining, but too beautiful to discard. Felt is pleasing to work with because of its opaque color and tidy edges, which do not require a hem; you can easily add a decorative edge with pinking or scalloped shears. Gingham and grosgrain ribbons are congenial companions for a homey fabric like felt. And pretty ribbons can be draped, looped, stitched, or tied into bows to become ornaments all by themselves. ✳ Fabric can deliver a powerful jolt of color to any ornament or decoration—so plan your color scheme carefully. Use fabrics with contrasting textures in just one or two colors, or unify contrasting fabrics with a single shade of trim, like the silver ribbons and twines we used. Whatever fabrics and trimmings you choose, everything you make will brighten your rooms, and your spirits, with the color and warmth of the holidays.

FANCY STOCKINGS
These five Christmas stockings (opposite), made of satin, velvet, silvery ribbons and trims, and pearl beads, are keep-sakes-in-waiting, to be displayed—and filled with surprises—for years to come. The matching balls nestle in silver lusterware and mercury-glass bowls on the mantel, where a candlestick plays an elegant solo in front of a nine-teenth-century English mirror. No two ornaments need be exactly alike (left), but fabrics and trims should harmonize.

SEWING A VELVET STOCKING

a silver lattice studded with pearls

SUPPLIES Velvet (for stocking); crystal sheer or polyester organza (for lining); ¼" silver ribbon (for decorative grid); ½" silver ribbon for cuff; pearl beads; stocking template on page 131 (double the size of the template on a photocopier); tracing paper; sewing marking pencil or tailor's chalk; sewing shears (for cutting fabric); embroidery scissors (for cutting trimmings); straight pins; needle and thread; and a sewing machine.

MAKING THE STOCKING This project requires intermediate sewing skills. 1. Fold sheer lining fabric to a double thickness, and pin template to fabric. With a sewing marking pencil, trace stocking template on fabric; leaving an additional 1" all the way around, cut through both layers of fabric. Repeat for the velvet, with right sides facing. Pin and baste lining to wrong side of each piece of velvet, sewing ¾" out from traced line; do not stitch across stocking's opening. 2. To make the ribbon lattice, copy the template's grid on tracing paper. Center traced grid on right side of stocking's front piece for use as a guide. Cut ribbon for each line of the grid, allowing ribbon to extend to edges of fabric; beneath tracing paper, position ribbons in the lattice pattern, pinning down at each end and at each intersection. 3. Using 3 or 4 discreet stitches, hand-stitch ribbon through velvet and lining at ends and intersections. Position border ribbon 1" below edge of fabric at stocking's opening; using a sewing machine, top-stitch border ribbon through velvet and lining. Pin the back of the stocking to the front, right sides facing. Stitch along the drawn pencil line. Remove pins, and trim seams to ½". 4. So seams will lay smoothly, clip notches in fabric at curved edges, to about ¹⁄₁₆" from stitching. Lightly press the wrong sides with a medium-hot iron; do not steam. Turn stocking right-side out, and finger press along seams. 5. Holding the stocking from the inside, hand-stitch a pearl bead at each intersection of the ribbon lattice. To hem top, fold fabric down ½" to the inside of the stocking, and press. Fold another ½", and hand-tack with a cross-stitch or hemstitch. To form a loop for hanging, cut a 5" piece of the ½" ribbon, fold in half, and hand-stitch both ends to the inside top-right corner of the stocking.

TRIMMING TIPS Although the template on page 131 provides a grid only for the lattice-patterned stocking, you can easily adapt the above technique to create the four other stockings shown on page 51. For the two basket-weave stockings, position ribbons in horizontal and vertical lines, weaving them as you go, and stitch them at the ends and inconspicuous intersections. For the striped stocking, machine-stitch the ribbon and rickrack. For a polka-dot stocking, hand-stitch pom-poms, buttons, or fabric circles in a grid.

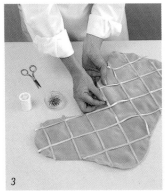

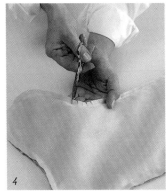

PINNING A SATIN ORNAMENT

ribbons, cords, and pearls, without sewing

 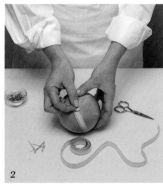 

SUPPLIES 2" and 3" Styrofoam balls; template on page 130 (reduce template to 90 percent on photocopier for 2" ball; enlarge to 125 percent for 3" ball); satin; metallic-silver ribbons, rickrack, and cord; fabric; straight pins; pearl-head pins; pearl beads; tassel balls; tassels; craft glue; Fray-Check; sewing shears (for cutting fabric); and embroidery scissors (for cutting trimmings). To make oversize ornaments, like our kissing ball on page 48, use larger Styrofoam balls; enlarge template on a photocopier to fit ball.

MAKING AN ORNAMENT Fabric-covered ornaments are easier to make than they look; assembling them is a great holiday project for kids who are old enough to work with pins. First, using the template, cut six sections of fabric for each ball. If you want to use two different fabrics on a single ornament, cut three sections of each fabric. Then: 1. Place one piece of fabric on the ball, stretching it pole to pole, and secure with a straight pin at each end. Place the second piece directly opposite the first, and secure it with one pin at each pole. Pieces should touch or slightly overlap at poles. Pin remaining four pieces of fabric in place so that the ball is com-

pletely covered. If the fabric overlaps on the sides, trim edges with embroidery scissors. 2. Leaving ribbon on spool, pin down one end at top pole. Wind ribbon all the way around ball, and pin again at top pole; cut loose ribbon, leaving enough overlap to cover first pin. Use a pin to secure ribbon at bottom pole. Repeat two more times, covering remaining seams. If ends of trimmings fray, carefully apply a dab of Fray-Check or craft glue. You may wish to add strips of silver twine to ball, centered on each section. To do so, wrap a length of twine around the ball for the measurement. Cut twine to correct measurement, dab craft glue on ends of twine to keep them from unraveling, and pin to ball at both poles; repeat on remaining sections. 3. To finish the top, stack a pearl, bead, or tassel ball on a pearl-head pin, then add a loop for hanging: Cut silver twine to desired length, dab glue on ends, and run pin through both ends of twine. Dip tip of pin in craft glue, and insert in ball; do not lift ball by loop until glue has dried completely. To finish bottom, add beads, pearls, or a tassel ball to pearl-head pin, dip tip of pin in glue, and insert; or finish with a tassel secured by a straight pin. You can embellish the sides by attaching a bead and sequin with a straight pin or pearl-head pin.

MAKING A FELT MINI STOCKING

a new way to fill an Advent calendar

SUPPLIES Felt; ribbon; template on page 130 (enlarge template to 125 percent on a photocopier); sewing marking pencil or tailor's chalk; sewing shears; pinking shears; sewing machine; straight pins; awl; and metal-rimmed tags.

SEWING A STOCKING 1. For each stocking, trace stocking template onto felt twice with a sewing marking pencil or tailor's chalk, and cut out shapes. 2. Pin the two pieces of felt together at the toe, heel, and instep. Cut a piece of ribbon just longer than the width of the stocking's opening; position about ¼" from top, and pin in place. Sewing ½" in from the edge, machine-stitch the front, back, and ribbon together; do not stitch stocking closed at top. 3. Trim around the seam with pinking shears. To hang the stocking, use an awl to punch a hole through both pieces of felt in the upper right corner; thread silver twine or a narrow ribbon through the holes, and tie on a metal-rimmed tag.

USING MINI STOCKINGS The charm of these little stockings is that it's easy to make a lot of them. They're just large enough to hold a small gift or sweet for each of the 24 days of Advent—or the 12 days of Christmas. If your tree is too small to hold 24 stockings, like our potted spruce (opposite), hang the rest from a ribbon swag; we used wire-edged ribbon so the garland's tails would hold their curls. An Advent tree can sit comfortably on a tabletop and brings a welcome Christmas aroma to a hall, foyer, or child's bedroom. We used a computer to print the numbers, then cut them out and glued them to tags. But you can label the tags by hand or with rubber stamps. For a lively tree, vary the colors of felt, and add ribbons in complementary patterns and hues. If you like, hang a swag of stockings without tags across a mantel. You can also tie stockings onto gifts, or use them to deliver party invitations or thank-you notes.

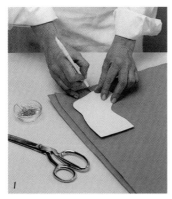

MAKING RIBBON FAVORS

pouches and cones for the table or tree

WIDE-RIBBON POUCHES These clever little sacks are easy to make and perform double duty, holding a small gift for each of the 24 days of Advent and trimming the tree (above left). Use wide grosgrain, taffeta, and satin ribbons in different colors and patterns (above right). Cut ribbon into 8" or 10" lengths, fold in half, and sew up sides on a machine, using contrasting or matching thread. Finish top edges with pinking shears, or fold top in half, and in half again, and snip diagonally to make large zigzags. Fill each bag with small goodies, like hard candies, and tie closed with silk cord. Tie a tag or vintage label to each present, and mark the appropriate date or number with rubber stamps, colorful crayons, or ink.

GROSGRAIN-RIBBON CONES Offering candy favors in these colorful cones is almost like giving bouquets. Cut a piece of 6"- or 8"-wide grosgrain ribbon to a 6" length; machine-stitch along cut edges to keep them from fraying. Roll the ribbon to form a cone shape. Hand-stitch to secure cone, or use fabric glue (above right), anchoring with a pin until glue dries. Fill cones with candy, like Jordan almonds or mints. Slip ribbon cones in fluted champagne glasses (right) to help ring in the New Year. Or sew a loop of heavy silver thread through a pearl bead and the pointy edge of cone's opening, and hang from a Christmas tree; stuff bottom of cone with tinsel or paper before adding candies so it will balance properly while hanging.

PUTTING UP A TREE

how to handle the season's centerpiece

CONSIDERING A TABLETOP TREE A small tree can be as memorable as an eight-footer. Whether you choose a live or cut tree, or an artificial one of goose feathers, it is easy and fun to decorate a little tree using a theme or a distinctive set of colors. A tabletop tree makes a handsome and long-lasting centerpiece, particularly desirable in a season when fresh flowers can be scarce and expensive. And because all their branches are near eye level, small trees are perfect for showing off your most intricate ornaments. Also, your decorations will be safe from small children and pets, provided the table is sufficiently tall.

SETTING UP A CUT TREE Although a large, fresh tree brings beauty and fragrance indoors, selecting and setting one up is a big project. These guidelines will make the task easier and neater, and help your tree last longer. First, choose a freshly cut tree that has not started to dry out. To check for freshness, hold a branch snugly between your thumb and forefinger several inches from the tip, then pull your hand toward the end. The branch should not lose many needles; if it does, look for another tree. To avoid leaving a trail of needles when you bring the tree into the house, wrap it in an old sheet. 1. Wrap a damp towel around the stump, and leave the tree in a cool but not freezing place until you are ready to put it up. 2. Use a saw to make a fresh cut about 1/2" above the base to remove any dried sap, which can prevent the tree from absorbing water. 3. Place the tree in the stand right away, and give it plenty of water. If more than a few hours go by, a new layer of sap can develop, and you will need to cut the trunk again. Choose a stand, like this aluminum one, with sturdy supports that adjust to fit any tree. Do not put the tree near a source of heat or ventilation, and make sure the bottom of the trunk is always immersed in water. Even if your stand holds a lot of water, remember to check it daily. 4. To make the clean-up process easier, place a plastic tree bag under the stand:

When it is time to take out the tree, just pull the bag up over the stand and the tree, and carry them outside; remove the bag and stand, then discard the tree. Or wrap the tree in the old sheet you used when you brought the tree indoors. 5. Use a tree skirt to hide the tree bag. Alternatively, hide the stand and bag in an attractive metal basin (6) or terra-cotta pot (7)—just make sure everything is secure and balanced.

BEADS

*Each a tiny joy, they light up every room
with their twinkle and luster*

Single glass beads can seem forlorn, as insignificant as grains of sand. But when strung together, beads become magical. They glisten like crystal, and when they harmonize, their dazzle can rival that of almost any jewel. Beads dress up everything they touch, and at Christmas they can transform your entire house, from the branches of a Christmas tree to the mirrors and window panes. ✳ Beads look as delicate as dewdrops yet can survive for thousands of years. It's easy to forget they're just tiny bits of glass. They come in such varied styles and colors, you can fashion anything, from beaded eggs tightly cocooned in strands of glittering rocailles to snowflakes that artfully blend tiny tri-cut beads with bugle beads and druks. Choosing glass beads is as enjoyable as shopping for jewelry. Look closely, and you'll discover each strain of bead has a distinct shape and sparkle. Rocailles are small glass beads with a square hole lined in silver. Tri-cut beads are tiny and faceted and have a round hole. Fire-polished crystal beads are faceted and can be large or small. Long bugle beads are usually faceted inside or outside. And druks are smooth, perfect spheres. The smallest beads usually appear as spacers in beaded jewelry and ornaments, but they can be used to great effect by themselves if a sufficient number are brought together. All of these styles are usually sold on "strands," which often come in "hanks" of ten to twelve. Big

SNOWFLAKE GARLAND
Beaded ornaments gain strength in numbers. This chain of snowflakes (opposite), lit softly by a candle in a 1920s sconce, twinkles against a lustrous silver-leaf mirror. Multicolored bells, balls, and candy canes (previous pages, left) are also dazzling in multiples; a goose-feather Christmas tree (previous pages, right) glistens with a colorful assortment. On the wall hangs a fresh Toyon-berry wreath.

bundles of hanks are called "bunches," but you won't see them very often in retail stores.
✳ Beadwork requires planning, time, and patience. You will probably want to start our intricate beaded wreath well before the holidays. But something simple, like a beaded monogram, can take as little as fifteen minutes to make, and allows for great

variation in the beads and colors you choose. Consider the traditional red or green of Christmas, or the white of snow, then try experimenting a little: A range of unusual greens or icy blues can add new, beautifully spirited tones to your decorations. ✳ Working with beads is satisfying. Beads are cool and pleasing to the touch, and make soothing, clicking sounds when they bump against one another. As you transfer them to wires and twist them into shape, it's tempting to think back to an earlier time when beads, often made from bear teeth and ostrich eggshells, were used as talismans by hunters and, later, as currency and objects of barter. Your beaded ornaments should last for decades. They will not fade, like textiles. If they get dirty or dull, gently wipe them with a damp cloth. And when the holidays are gone, wrap them carefully in tissue, and store them safely until next year. Your beaded heirlooms will twinkle for generations to come.

CRYSTAL SNOWFALL
Beaded ornaments don't have to hang on a tree. Each snowflake in this window (opposite) hangs from a pin threaded through a single druk bead. The snowflakes were inspired by late-nineteenth-century ornaments made in Czechoslovakia and exported to the United States. Like real snowflakes, no two need be alike; combine clear beads as you wish. Placed near a window, a tree with widely spaced branches (left) allows beaded ornaments to shine in the sunlight.

WIRING BEADS ON A FORM

monograms, candy canes, and snowflakes

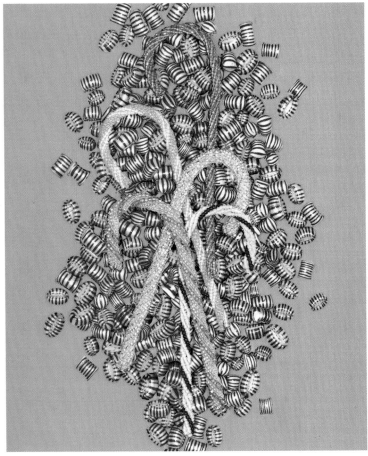

SUPPLIES To make the ornaments in this chapter, you'll need (opposite, top left): Strands of beads (buy them in hanks or bunches; loose beads can be used to make the snowflakes); assorted gauges (20 to 34) of tinned copper wire; round-nosed pliers (for making loops in wire); flat-nosed pliers (for refining wired shapes or flattening wire loops); side cutters (for cutting wire); scissors; and masking tape.

TRANSFERRING BEADS TO WIRE This is the first step in making these beaded monograms, candy canes, and bells. Open the spool of wire, and cut the open wire at an angle. Carefully take one strand of beads from the bunch, and tape one end to the work surface. Pulling strand taut, transfer strung beads to the wire by feeding the wire through the holes (opposite, bottom). Slide the beads down the wire toward the spool. When you have transferred the number of beads you need, crimp the end of the wire so the beads will not slide off.

MONOGRAMS Beaded monograms are an elegant way to personalize wrapped gifts (above left); you can also hang them on a Christmas tree or a wreath. We used rocailles to make our monograms. First, find a script letter you like in a font book (or a printed advertisement). Enlarge letter on a photocopier. Cut 20-gauge wire to size: We found 18" to be a good length. Make a loop at one end with round-nosed pliers. Transfer enough beads to fill the entire letter, leaving about 3" of wire unbeaded to allow for sharp turns in the shape, and loop the wire. Using the enlarged letter as a template, shape the beaded wire. Cut off excess beads and wire at one end, leaving about ½" to ¾" exposed wire, and loop it. Use extra 20-gauge wire for a hook. Some letters must be made in two pieces, like P (below left); lash pieces together with 30-gauge wire.

CANDY CANES We made candy canes out of rocaille and tri-cut beads. You can combine colors or make solid-colored canes (opposite, right). A four-strand candy cane in red, green, and white, for instance, will be composed of two wires with white beads, one wire with green beads, and one wire with red beads. A five-strand cane in red and white (far right) has four wires with white beads and one wire with red beads. Use only one kind of bead on each wire. First, cut either four or six pieces

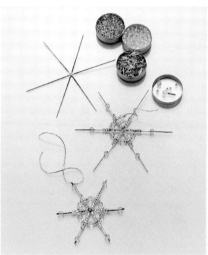

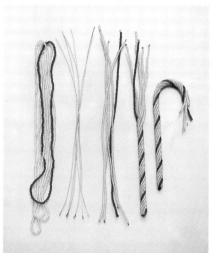

of 24-gauge wire into 7½" lengths. Using round-nosed pliers, make a tiny loop at one end of each wire. Transfer enough beads from their strings to fill each wire; leave just enough room to loop the open end of the wire, preventing beads from slipping off. The beads should be slightly loose on the wire. Once all the wires are beaded, shape them into a candy cane by holding the wires together at one end and twisting them together; keep the beaded wires even and the surface smooth. Bend wires at the top into the gentle hook of a cane. Some ends will be uneven; you can adjust them by removing a few beads where necessary and making those wires shorter.

SNOWFLAKES Use a premade snowflake form (see the Guide), or join three lengths of 20-gauge wire by soldering or lashing with 30-gauge wire. To make the snowflake pictured (top right), transfer four 5/o rocailles to one arm; wrap one end of a 12" length of 24-gauge wire on arm, as close to last bead as possible. Thread a large druk bead, a smaller one, and a large one onto wire; repeat bead transfer on next arm, and tie wire close to last bead. Repeat until an inner perimeter is formed, then add two 5/o rocailles, a bugle bead, and a large druk bead to each arm. Loop end of each arm closed. To make a garland, attach loops with wire or small jump rings.

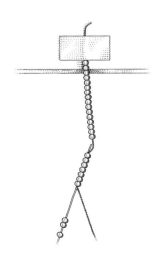

WRAPPING STRANDS ON A FORM

bells, balls, and eggs

BELLS To make a medium bell (1¾" in diameter at base), transfer 81" (about four and one-half strands) of small beads (such as rocailles or tri-cuts) to 30-gauge wire (see page 64). Crimp the open end of wire, leaving about an inch of lead wire at that end. Then cut the beaded wire off the spool, and crimp second end. Mark four spots at 90-degree increments on the inside lip of a bell mold (see the Guide); the marks will indicate where the beaded wires will be sewn together once they've been wrapped around the mold (top left). 1. Insert a skewer (or dowel) into the hole at top of bell mold, using a T pin to secure it in place. Wrap the unbeaded lead wire around the T pin until the beads are snug on wire. Begin wrapping beads around the mold, being sure the beads are tight against each other and flush against the mold. Continue wrapping until the entire mold is covered.

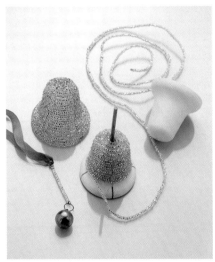

2. Tape end of wire firmly in place on the inside bottom edge of mold. Starting at the top of the bell, secure four strips of tape to the beaded wires, ending each strip on the inside of the mold, about halfway up the side. Using 34-gauge wire threaded through a small sewing needle, stitch the rows of beads together, starting at one of the marks on the base of the bell form. Loop the wire around each row of beads (see inset illustration), pulling each loop closed with pliers. Continue sewing up side of the bell, being careful to keep wire straight and untwisted; small kinks can cause the wire to break. Stitch the three other seams, using the marks as a guide and removing the tape as you sew. Upon reaching the top of the bell with the fourth seam, keep the needle threaded, and set it aside for the moment. Unwrap the wire from the T pin, and remove the pin. Remove beaded bell by sliding it off the form. To finish the top and bottom of bell, straighten the loop at the end of the wire, and loop the wire around the previous row of beads. 3. To make the clapper, cut a small piece of 22-gauge wire (its length should equal the height of the bell, plus 2"). Using round-nosed pliers, bend one end of the wire into a medium-size loop (about ⅛"). Slip one 8-millimeter bead onto wire (bead must be larger than opening left in top of bell); add sixteen 10/o silver-lined rocailles, and close with another loop. Add a glass ball to bottom. (We used balls ranging in size from ⅜" to ½".) You may need to adjust the number of rocailles on wire in order to make the bottom three-quarters of ball visible. 4. Tie ribbon through loop at top of wire, and thread ribbon through hole at top of bell. Take up the threaded needle, and stitch directly across the opening of bell, threading the medium loop at the top of clapper wire in the process. Clip any excess seam wire. Consider making bells in different sizes and harmonious colors (left) to hang on a door, window, or mirror.

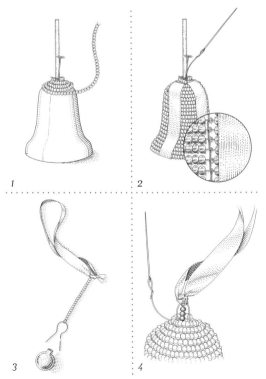

1

2

3

4

BALLS Use strands of rocailles or tri-cuts to wrap balls. With a hat pin, poke a hole through the center of a Styrofoam ball and out the other side (above left). Use the pin as a handle while working. Starting at middle, paint ball liberally with craft glue. Let glue set 2 to 3 minutes, or until tacky. Wrap a string of beads around equator of ball, anchoring bare string at beginning and end of strand into glue. Work toward one pole. At end of a string, begin laying another; avoid gaps by lining up ends of strings. For striped balls, alternate colors or kinds of beads when laying new string. Begin and finish each new color on the back, aligning vertically. Repeat until ball is covered. Cut excess beads from ends. Finish the bottom by stacking larger beads of your choice on a flat pin; glue pin into the bottom of ball. Finish the top with a 1½" piece of 24-gauge wire looped on one end. Choose a matching, larger bead, and transfer it to the wire; then glue the beaded wire into top of ball with the loop side facing out. Once glue has dried thoroughly, thread a hook or ribbon through loop. If desired, attach a beaded leaf (see page 69) to ball.

EGGS To blow out an egg, poke pinholes close together at the ends of the shell; gently break bits between pinholes to make one large hole. Stir insides with a toothpick or long needle, then, with your mouth or a rubber ear syringe, blow the insides into a bowl. Rinse and dry egg shell. Cut a piece of 24-gauge wire 8" long, loop one end, and thread through holes in egg (above right); make another loop so egg won't slide off. Use wire as a handle while working. Following the same process used for making ball ornaments, wrap beads around egg, being careful not to crush it. Finish top and bottom of egg with larger beads threaded on the wire that's been passed through the egg; make a new loop on each end of the wire. Attach a hook or ribbon, for hanging, to the top loop.

MAKING AN HEIRLOOM WREATH

beaded leaves and pearl berries

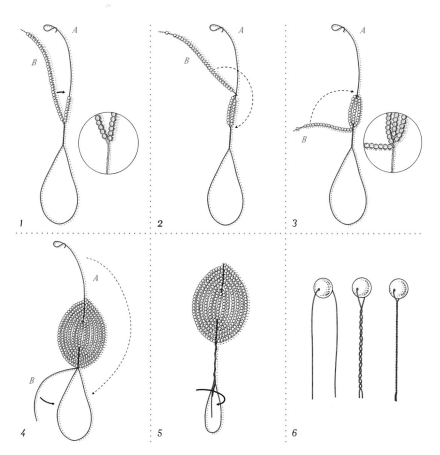

MAKING THE LEAVES To make the wreath, you'll need 78 leaves, half of them slightly larger than the other half. To make a single leaf, begin by transferring three strands of silver-lined iris 10/o rocailles to 26-gauge tinned copper wire (see page 65), leaving one end of wire attached to spool. Then make a loop in the open end of wire, and move nine beads to within 6" of loop; this set of beads will be called the basic beads (for basic count) in following instructions. Hold wire with both hands, keeping it straight and taut in front of you. Hold basic beads in place with your left thumb and forefinger; hold beads near spool in place with your right thumb and forefinger. At this point there should be a gap of at least 8" of bare wire between basic beads and rest of beads. 1. Bringing forefingers together, transfer basic beads to right hand, while twisting the gap of wire together with left hand. Twist wire very tightly four or five times (see inset illustration) just below beads in right hand. Then lift the beaded wire (labeled B) toward left side of basic beads (labeled A). 2. To create leaf with a pointed tip, follow this procedure from this step forward when adding a row to right side of basic beads: Wrap B around A just above topmost basic bead (from this point on, wrap wire around front, to back, and around front again).

Add two beads to basic-bead count, and, with B and A at a 45-degree angle to each other (as shown), push beads on B down wire firmly into place. 3. Bring B down along right side of basic beads. Wrap B around wire at bottom of beads, and bring strand of wires up along left side of the developing leaf. 4. Continue forming leaf until it has desired number of rows. Then unroll 6" of wire from spool, snip it, and twist B around the wire beneath leaf. Bring A down back center of leaf; tuck it inside loop. 5. Continue twisting wire down loop, closing it up and creating a straight "stem."

WIRING THE PEARL BERRIES You will need 39 pearl berries. To make them, cut a piece of 28-gauge tinned copper wire to a length of 10". Thread a 6-millimeter pearl bead through the wire, and center it on the wire (see illustration 6). Fold wire down and around pearl so both sides meet directly under the bead. Twist wire together evenly by holding two ends together in one hand while twisting the bead with your other hand.

ASSEMBLING THE WREATH Group the leaves into 26 bunches of three leaves each. Alternate small and large leaves within each bunch. Wrap stems of each bunch four or five times with 28-gauge tinned copper wire. Set aside. Group the pearls into bunches of three using the same method. Cut a piece of 19-gauge nickel silver wire (or a wire hanger) to a length of 27½". Shape it into a circle, overlapping the ends by 1". Using 28-gauge wire, tightly wrap ends together, producing a secure, closed circle. Twist wire to make a loop to hang the wreath. Begin placing bunches of leaves on the frame, wrapping each stem tightly to the frame three or four times. Add a second bunch of leaves to cover stems of previous bunch; secure those stems to frame. After attaching two bunches of leaves, lay a bunch of pearl berries on frame; secure with wire. Repeat (right) until the wreath is completed, remembering to insert berries on top of every second bunch of leaves. Using wire-mesh ribbon, tie a bow, and secure it to bottom of wreath using 28-gauge wire.

GINGERBREAD

*A wonderful blend of sugar and spice
that's perfect for adorning the tree—
and almost everything else in the house*

If there's one food that embodies Christmas to perfection, it's gingerbread. Bake it, and your entire house smells like a holiday. Nibble it, and you're transported to Christmas past. But what elevates gingerbread above a mere seasonal treat is its decorative quality. Turn it into ornaments and gifts, and every tree or tabletop it touches seems joyous. Even its monkish hue, which may not look very festive, is a warm and amiable backdrop for whimsical shapes and fanciful icing in any color you like. ✳ The gingerbread cookie was the favorite Christmas treat of early-American children. It became popular because it was inexpensive to make and resilient enough to withstand the vagaries of wood- and coal-fired ovens. Gingerbread enthusiasts, however, like to point out that gingerbread became beloved for its taste—that inimitable combination of molasses, ginger, cinnamon, and nutmeg—and for the fun it provides. ✳ Gingerbread's delights were evident as far back as the early Christian era, when ancient Romans baked it in portable ovens. The confection was so desirable during the reign of Elizabeth I that the royal family employed its own gingerbread baker. Gingerbread became synonymous with extravagant decoration; cut into shapes or baked in wooden molds, it was iced with sugar and gilded. Gingerbread also proved to be a near-perfect construction medium, ideal for building elaborate edifices like the one that

EDIBLE ORNAMENTS
A nineteenth-century English transferware platter (opposite) shimmers above gingerbread snowflakes and a house with caramelized-sugar windows. The gingham bow is purely decorative; the platter is hung with a plate hanger. Iced gingerbread cookies adorn a Christmas tree (previous pages, left and right). To make them, enlarge the templates on pages 134 and 135, and trace them on cardboard, then on dough. Holes are made in cookies, for hanging, before they're baked.

bedazzled Hansel and Gretel and that inspires us as gingerbread artists to this day. ✳ Creating a gingerbread house or Christmas-tree decorations can be so enjoyable, you may want to make it a part of your holiday activities each year. The fun begins with the planning. You can render, in miniature, your favorite cottage or skyscraper, or perhaps a facade of your house—or the house of your dreams. Or you might consult an architecture or history book for more ideas. Stars, butterflies, and snowflakes make enchanting decorations, too. Gingerbread is so adaptable—almost anything you like can be interpreted with golden-brown dough and royal icing, from barnyard animals to Fabergé eggs. ✳ Even as a building material, gingerbread abounds with sensual delights. There's the pleasure of rolling the dough and cutting out designs. There's comfort and delight in the scent of baking gingerbread, redolent of spices, as it wafts from the oven and fills the kitchen and house. Making gingerbread is an engaging holiday project for any child old enough to manipulate a cookie cutter or squeeze a pastry bag with some degree of precision. And decorating cookies is a splendid exercise in self-expression, especially because icing is so forgiving; if you make a mistake, just wipe it off before it dries, and try again. Gingerbread cookies and constructions can be elegantly simple or astonishingly complex, and each has its own reward. But gingerbread, of course, is meant to be eaten, so be sure to make an extra batch or two. You will recall that heavenly flavor each time you admire your gingerbread house or gaze at the colorful cookies glistening on the tree.

NOAH'S ARK TREE
Because gingerbread can be cut in any shape and frosted in any color, a tree trimmed with gingerbread ornaments can tell a story or impart a theme. Animals adorn the branches of this staunch fir topped with a cookie star (opposite). The cookies are iced in soft winter hues inspired by the eucalyptus, seeded eucalyptus, Acacia baileyana, and santolina of the lush, fragrant garland framing the window.

CRISP GINGERBREAD COOKIES

MAKES 16 LARGE COOKIES

6 cups sifted all-purpose flour
1 teaspoon baking soda
$\frac{1}{2}$ teaspoon baking powder
1 cup (2 sticks) unsalted butter
1 cup dark-brown sugar, packed
4 teaspoons ground ginger
4 teaspoons ground cinnamon
1 $\frac{1}{2}$ teaspoons ground cloves
1 $\frac{1}{2}$ teaspoons salt
1 teaspoon finely ground pepper
2 large eggs
1 cup unsulfured molasses

BAKING DAY Making gingerbread with family or friends is the perfect winter activity. Martha's friend Lara Pasternak rolls out dough on a Silpat baking mat, then presses a cookie cutter into the dough (top row). After the cookies have cooled (bottom row), Lara and Martha decorate them with royal icing tinted in a variety of colors.

1. In a large bowl, sift together the flour, baking soda, and baking powder. Set aside.
2. In the bowl of an electric mixer, cream butter and brown sugar until fluffy. Mix in the spices, salt, and pepper; add eggs and molasses. Add in flour mixture on low speed. Divide dough into thirds; wrap in plastic. Chill at least 1 hour.
3. Heat oven to 350°. On a floured work surface, roll out dough $\frac{1}{8}$ inch thick. Cut into desired shapes. Transfer to baking sheets lined with Silpat mats (see Baking Tips); refrigerate until firm, 15 minutes. Bake 8 to 10 minutes, or until crisp but not darkened. Cool on wire racks, and decorate.

BAKING TIPS: You can roll out dough on a cutting board, a baking sheet, or on marble, but perhaps the best surface is a Silpat baking mat—a French nonstick mat used by professional bakers (see the Guide). A Silpat can be transferred directly to a baking sheet so you will not have to struggle moving the raw dough or worry that the sheet's imperfect surface will affect the cookies. The cookies will come out smooth and even, and will look as if they were made by a professional. Always work with cookie dough that has been chilled at least 20 minutes; otherwise the dough will be too sticky and soft to cut. Be sure to roll out dough so it is no thicker than $\frac{1}{8}$ inch; otherwise your cookies will be too heavy to use as ornaments on a tree. Remove the excess dough after cutting, and save it to make more cookies.

ROYAL ICING

MAKES ABOUT 2½ CUPS

2 large egg whites, or 5 tablespoons meringue powder mixed with a scant $\frac{1}{2}$ cup water
1 pound confectioners' sugar
Food coloring

In the bowl of an electric mixer, beat egg whites, sugar, and 2 teaspoons water on low speed for 10 minutes. Add food coloring, a little at a time, to achieve desired color. Royal icing needs to have different consistencies, depending on how you use it. For piping, the icing should easily pass through a pastry tip and retain its shape. For spreading, also known as floodwork, icing should have the consistency of squeeze-bottle mustard. Icing is perfect for floodwork if you can lift your spatula and see a ribbonlike trail for 5 seconds. If icing is too thin, beat 2 to 3 minutes more; if it is too thick, add water a few drops at a time, mixing thoroughly between additions. NOTE: Raw eggs should not be used in food prepared for pregnant women, babies, young children, the elderly, or anyone whose health is compromised; use meringue-powder substitute instead.

GETTING READY TO ICE *To decorate cookies you will need: Royal icing; several 10- or 12-inch-tall clear-plastic pastry bags; couplers; #2, #3, and #5 plain decorating tips; a pastry brush (or a sable paintbrush for small cookies); an offset metal spatula (or a table knife); toothpicks; tall drinking glasses; twist ties; paper towels; sanding or regular sugar; and powdered or paste food coloring. Because food coloring is extremely potent, use it sparingly. Start by placing a smidgen of paste or a few grains of powder on the end of a toothpick, and mix into the icing; add more as needed. To color sugar, pour it in a resealable plastic bag, add a pinch of powdered food coloring, seal, and shake.*

ANIMAL SNOWSCAPE *This lighthearted centerpiece is made with gingerbread animals, not all of them creatures of icy habitats, standing in snowlike sugar in a large glass canister; this one was probably once used in a pharmacy. To decorate the cookies, apply a base layer of royal icing with a pastry bag and a #5 tip, then spread evenly with an offset metal spatula, and let dry. The icing should have a smooth, creamy consistency for floodwork. To create large designs, you will need a #2 tip and icing with a thicker consistency. While the designs are still wet, use sanding sugar, which has a large grain, to flock the wet parts of the icing, giving the cookie a sparkling, multidimensional appearance. After the cookies are flocked, shake or brush them to remove excess sugar.*

CREATING DECORATIONS WITH GINGERBREAD

techniques for icing cookies and making a wreath

ICING TIPS Before you begin working, remove your watch, rings, bracelets, and any other jewelry that might inhibit your decorating or become encrusted. Start by attaching the proper tip—#2 for piping, #5 for floodwork on large cookies, #3 for floodwork on small cookies—to a pastry bag fitted with a coupler. Form a cuff by turning down the top three inches of the bag. Place the empty bag upright in a tall drinking glass. Spoon the icing into the bag until it is one-half to two-thirds full, and close with a twist tie. Fill all the bags you will need. Remove the filled bag from the drinking glass for a moment, and place a damp paper towel in the bottom of the glass; put the bag, tip-side down, back in the glass. The damp paper towel prevents the icing from drying and clogging the tip. Alternatively, put a toothpick in the end of each pastry tip to prevent clogging. Icing will keep overnight—and for several days—either way. If the colors start to separate, gently

massage the bag to remix the icing. Once you have finished decorating your cookies, store them in an airtight container between layers of waxed paper or parchment paper. If you are traveling with cookies, place a thin sheet of Bubble Wrap between the layers.

ICING AND FLOCKING These techniques can be used to decorate any of the gingerbread cookies shown on these pages. First bake Crisp Gingerbread Cookies, and let them cool; make Royal Icing (recipes, page 76). 1. Outline half a cookie with the piping icing using a #2 tip. Turn the cookie 180 degrees, and pipe the other half. Let the icing set, 5 to 10 minutes. 2. Using the flooding icing and a #5 tip, draw zigzags on the cookie's surface. 3. Spread the icing evenly

over the entire cookie with an offset metal spatula. Let the cookie dry overnight, and store the icing as recommended above. 4. When the floodwork is dry, use a #2 tip to pipe your chosen design. Here, we're making a leafy vine motif. First, pipe wavy horizontal lines on each cookie, starting at the top, to make the vines. Next add the leaves: Apply pressure to the pastry bag to make a leaf's base, and let up on the pressure as you move toward the tip. Alternate leaves on either side of the vine. If you want to apply silver dragées, do so before the icing hardens. 5. To flock the cookie: While the icing is still soft, hold the cookie over a clean paper towel or baking sheet, and sprinkle it liberally with sanding sugar. Let the cookie sit for 5 minutes, then shake off any excess sugar onto the paper towel or baking sheet. Let the icing and sugar dry, about half an hour, and remove any stray crystals with a pastry brush or paintbrush. Shake any sugar that has fallen onto the paper towel back into the bowl to reuse. 6. If you don't want to cover the entire surface of the cookie with icing, you can let the gingerbread itself be the background. Pipe the outline and the pattern with a #2 tip. When dry, fill in alternating sections of pattern with flooding icing, using a #3 tip. The icing should be fluid enough to fill in the design without using a spatula. 7. Sprinkle with sugar. Let dry, and shake off any excess sugar.

BAKING A COOKIE WREATH Make one recipe Crisp Gingerbread Cookie dough (recipe, page 76); roll it out onto a well-floured work surface. Cut about sixty leaf shapes from the dough (we used two different cutters; see the Guide), and place the leaves on a parchment-lined baking sheet. Refrigerate until chilled, about 20 minutes. Using the back of a paring knife, press "vein" patterns into each leaf (below left). Line another baking sheet with parchment. Using a dinner plate or a cake pan as a template, draw an 8- or 9-inch circle on the paper. Place the leaves around the circle (below right), brushing a bit of water with a pastry brush onto the back of each leaf before placing it over the next one. Overlap and stagger the leaves in the form of a wreath. Chill the wreath, about 20

minutes. Heat the oven to 350 degrees, and bake the wreath until crisp but not darkened, 12 to 15 minutes. Transfer to a wire rack, and let cool overnight. To decorate, stand wreath against your arm at an angle, and sprinkle with confectioners' sugar put through a sieve. Better yet, have someone use both hands to hold wreath at an angle while you work. The sugar on top of the gingerbread leaves will look as natural as fresh snowfall. Attach a bow, and hang away from heat or moisture.

STOCKING GIFTS *Gingerbread cookies are always welcome gifts. Tied in cellophane bags with red-ribbon knots, these stocking cookies (above) stay fresh and are festive adornments for a mantel or dinner table. Pipe guests' initials on the stockings, and use the cookies as place cards that also serve as sweet favors.*

COOKIE WREATH *Almost any holiday icon can be interpreted in gingerbread. A wreath (opposite) is made by overlapping cookies and baking all of them at once, with a final snowlike dusting of confectioners' sugar.*

SNOWFLAKES *You can embellish any corner of a house with gingerbread cookies. These snowflakes rest on a mantel arrayed with greenery, pewter candlesticks, and silver-glass balls. The cookies are decorated with silver dragées and flocked icing; the contrast of snow-white icing and gingerbread brown is quite dramatic. Although you probably will want to discard your gingerbread decorations after the holiday season, they will last long past Christmas Day if you keep them away from moisture and heat—and if no one eats them.*

BUILDING A GOTHIC COTTAGE

the quickest way to have a gingerbread house

BAKING THE WALLS Make two batches of Crisp Gingerbread Cookie dough (recipe, page 76), flatten it, and wrap it in cellophane. Refrigerate until chilled so dough won't be sticky, about 20 minutes. Roll half the dough onto a well-floured Silpat baking mat, and place the template for the facade on top. (The templates are on pages 134 and 135; you'll need to enlarge them on a photocopier.) Roll out the rest of the dough, and cover with templates for the sides. 1. With a paring knife, cut out the facade and sides, and remove excess dough with an offset metal spatula. Place the Silpats on two baking sheets, and refrigerate until chilled so dough will retain its shape, about 20 minutes. Heat oven to 350 degrees, and bake until the facade and sides are crisp and the edges turn golden brown, about 10 to 12 minutes. Transfer to wire racks, and let cool overnight.

DECORATING THE HOUSE Make Royal Icing for piping (recipe, page 76). Using a #2 tip on a pastry bag, pipe outlines of house. If a squiggle goes awry, scrape off icing before it dries, and apply again. If you wish to fill in the roof tiles or other areas, wait for piping to dry, then apply flooding icing where you desire, using a #3 tip. If you want to flock only the roof or other areas with sugar, make sure icing on these areas is soft; the icing on the

rest of house must already be dry. 2. Hold house over a clean baking sheet, and sprinkle liberally with sanding sugar. Let house stand for 5 minutes, then shake off any excess sugar onto baking sheet. Let icing and sugar dry, about 1 hour; remove any stray crystals with a pastry brush or paintbrush. To attach sides, which support the facade like an easel, pipe icing along the edges of facade. Then "glue" both sides in place, propping them up with bowls until icing dries, about 2 hours to overnight. For the windows, make panes of caramelized sugar: Stir 1½ cups sugar, ¼ cup water, and 1 teaspoon lemon juice in a heavy-bottomed saucepan; melt over high heat, pushing sugar around with the back of a wooden spoon. Mixture will turn brown in about 3 to 4 minutes. Remove from heat when soft cracks appear in sugar and a candy thermometer registers 282 degrees. 3. On a Silpat or nonstick baking sheet, pour puddles large enough to fill windows; let cool until hardened. 4. Lift panes off Silpat; attach to back of windows with royal icing. You can illuminate windows with votives or tiny electric lights; just be sure to keep them from touching the house.

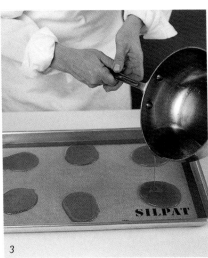

part 3

SET THE TABLE

YOUR FINEST PLATES
AND GLASSES AND NAPKINS
CRAVE A PLACE
AT THE TABLE ONCE AGAIN.
WELCOME THEM BACK.
LET THEM SPARKLE.
IN A MAGICAL ROOM,
THE SIMPLEST MEAL BECOMES
A MEMORABLE GIFT.
BUT BE GENEROUS WITH
COLORFUL FRUITS
AND SWEET DESSERTS.
THEY ARE THE
VERY VISION, AND TASTE, OF
CHRISTMAS DAY.

GLITTER &
GILDING

*A dusting or a burnish
is all it takes to bring winter's
glamour to a holiday table*

Nature understands the importance of sparkle, particularly in winter, when the landscape is bewitchingly monochromatic. Think of the tiny rainbows glinting on an icicle or the sugary sparkles in snow, then imagine how flat everything would look without the twinkle. Indoors, the glittering edges and muted hues of winter can be wonderfully evocative. They can remind you of a frosty Christmas morning long ago. They can call to mind the romance of a fresh snowfall, even if you live in the tropics. ✳ A table starts to shine the moment you set out your crystal and china, but to make it truly glitter and glow, why not add some real glitter? The best kind to use is made from ground Mylar and looks like colored sand. It can be ravishing when sprinkled like a dusting of snow on objects from nature, such as nuts and pinecones. Silver and gold glitters are the perfect accompaniments for a table clothed in winter whites, but glitter comes in a great array of colors. You can use one color alone, or blend two or three together to create exactly the tone you want. To dull the brilliance of silver glitter, for example, add some pewter gran- ules. There are also larger-grain glitters, which come in a variety of sheens and can even be translucent; just don't mix them with fine- grain glitter. ✳ Too much glitter can seem garish, so it's best to use glittered decorations sparingly, like a potent spice. Glittered nuts look magical when mixed with unembellished nuts and painted-

PINECONE TASSEL
Glitter is prettiest when you use just a little. A sprinkling graces the edges of three large ponderosa pinecones (opposite), which are fitted with eye screws and tied to a silver sconce with silver- metallic ribbon. The walnuts and almonds clad in silvers and golds (previous pages, left and right) sparkle brightest when used alongside the rough shells of undecorated nuts in a simple centerpiece.

silver leaves in a clear-glass compote. Our glittered projects are easy to make, and can be fun to create with children. But working with glitter can be messy, so spread out craft paper or paper towels before you begin—you don't want every surface in your house to sparkle. ✳ Gilding is the lustrous companion to glitter. Gilded decorations, like the artificial fruit used in our centerpieces, gleam with a sleek, polished finish. You can wrap almost any smooth surface in a thin layer of metallic leaf, which is affixed with an adhesive and then burnished with a brush or soft cloth. We covered polystyrene fruit in silver leaf, aluminum leaf, and green-mint and aqua metallic leaf—icy, luminous colors to lighten the season's dark days. Metallic leaf usually comes in "books" made up of twenty-five paper-thin "leaves" in one of numerous sizes. Silver leaf is 3¾ inches square. Aluminum leaf measures 5½ inches square. And colored metallic leaf imported from Japan, sold in books of one hundred, is 4⁵⁄₁₆ inches square. Although true silver leaf tarnishes, it will retain its polish for years if treated with a sealant such as Ronan Acrylic

Clear Overcoat. ✳ Touches of glitter and gilding can go almost anywhere. We hung large glittered pinecones from a silver sconce, set gilded fruit in a greenery wreath, and tied our "silver" wishbones onto little gifts. The fun of glitter and gilding, after all, is that it can surprise us—and a winter house should be filled with surprises.

ENHANCING ORNAMENTS
You can decorate almost any decoration by applying extra glitter yourself. To complement the patina of antique ornaments, like those on this goose-feather tree (opposite), use pewter and bronze glitters. Or, you can coat entire ornaments (see page 95). Antique tinsel garlands swagged on the mirror have a patina all their own. To make "silver" napkin rings (below), save wishbones from roast chickens, and spray them with chrome paint. String silver cord from tip to tip, wrap it six times around each one, and tie off the cord.

Layers of textures and sheen in silver create a graceful setting for a Christmas or New Year's Eve supper. A cloth made of sheer-silver silk organza and edged with wide antique silver ribbon (opposite) is draped over a nineteenth-century oval American Empire table with a lyre base, painted white. The turn-of-the-century Swedish settee, also painted white, provides guests with intimate seating. The photographs hang from linen ribbon cords attached to a picture molding.

SILVER DETAILS

Instead of using traditional candlesticks, stand thin white candles in antique blown-glass cordials filled with tiny silver dragées (above left). Be sure to pour in enough dragées to hold the candle upright. At the center of each Wedgwood luster-ware plate (left), a place card waits in a silver holder. The deckle-edged card is hand-lettered with silver ink; a hole punched near the top of the card provides a place for a knotted silver ribbon.

FROSTED HOLLY *Bring a holiday feeling to a ledge or mantel with several long sprigs of dried holly edged in silver glitter, a silver lusterware bowl filled with miniature glittered pinecones, and a selection of silver-glass Christmas-tree ornaments. The holly branches stand in a mismatched collection of new and antique glass bottles and vases.*

DECORATING WITH GLITTER

pinecones, holly, nuts, and glass ornaments

SUPPLIES To make the glittered decorations in this chapter, you will need craft glue; a small paintbrush; small bowls; and fine-grain glitter. Use single colors of glitter, or mix them to achieve the color or effect you want. Because working with glitter can get messy, cover your work surface with craft paper or paper towels. To let glittered decorations dry, set them on a sheet of craft paper or on a hard surface, like a glass bowl.

PINECONES To "frost" a small pinecone, brush a thin layer of glue down the pinecone's outer edges (above left). Then roll pinecone in bowl of glitter until all the glue is coated. Let dry. To add glitter to a large pinecone, apply glue and glitter in sections; otherwise, some of the glue will dry before you can apply glitter. Brush a thin layer of glue onto a section of pinecone's tips (above center), then use your fingers to sprinkle on glitter. Hold pinecone over bowl of glitter to catch any stray sparkles. After each application of glitter, check to make certain edges are covered. To hang a pinecone tassel (see page 88), use an awl to start a hole in the stem end of each pinecone, and screw in an eye screw, through which you can thread ribbon, twine, or wire.

HOLLY Dried holly leaves can be used individually or in arrangements, on wreaths, as place cards, or tied to wrapped gifts. Working on one holly leaf at a time, brush a thin layer of glue along the outer edges of the leaf

(above right). Holding holly over bowl of glitter, use your fingers to sprinkle glitter onto glue. Let the glue dry completely. To make the glittered holly wreath that's hung above the dessert table on page 116, apply glitter to the leaves on three- or four-leaf sprigs of dried holly. Using 28-gauge floral wire, attach sprigs to an 18" double-wire wreath form. Beginning at the bottom of the wreath, work up either side, pointing all the leaves upward, until they meet at top. Tie a bow with long streamers at bottom.

NUTS AND GLASS ORNAMENTS To decorate any kind of nut or glass Christmas-tree ornament (left), brush a thin layer of glue over entire surface, then roll in glitter until coated; let dry. With glass ornaments, you may need to apply the glue and glitter one section at a time. This is a great way to transform flea-market finds.

SILVER FRUIT WREATH
Gilded artificial fruit adds lus-
ter to a wreath of shiny dark-
green camellia leaves dressed
up with a silver-mesh bow. The
fruit is wired into the finished
greenery wreath. On the mantel,
a nineteenth-century black-
marble case clock is flanked by
matching glass compotes piled
high with antique glass orna-
ments. A pair of vases holds
pale-peach amaryllis, Star of
Bethlehem, and eucalyptus.
A swag of eucalyptus, seeded
eucalyptus, Acacia baileyana,
and santolina curves below.

HOLLY PLACE CARD *The pointy edges and muted color of these dried holly leaves were*
inspiration for a place setting in pale greens and whites. With thin silver cord threaded onto a
needle, the stem of the glittered holly sprig is stitched four times onto the place card, creating
the little collar. The setting uses an antique French salad plate and reticulated bread plate and
a pale-green Wedgwood dinner plate. The octagonal Venetian-glass goblet echoes the salad plate.

A NEW CHRISTMAS COLOR *All the details in this room harmonize to create an unexpected holiday color scheme. The familiar reds and greens are here, but muted, and cooled by touches of ice-blue glass and china. How many trees can a dining room have? One as a centerpiece (detail, opposite) and a second on a tabletop, with iced-gingerbread animal cookies.*

PINECONE PLACE CARD *An evergreen sprig and miniature glittered pinecones form a simple place-card holder. Hot glue is used to attach the pinecones to the sprig; the needles anchor the place card. Antique-glass pieces and a Wedgwood dish outlined in creamy "icicles" add accents of wintry blue; their colors are intensified by the subtle shades of the two lusterware plates and the linen tablecloth.*

POTTED SILVER TOPIARY *To make a decoration reminiscent of an opulent, old-fashioned sterling-silver centerpiece, we gilded polystyrene apples and pears in various sizes with aluminum leaf. The fruit is hot-glued to a Styrofoam cone; sprigs of eucalyptus fill in the spaces. The clay pot is sprayed with silver paint, and live moss nestles around the trunk. The tree can last for years: Remove dried sprigs before storing; the next season, insert fresh sprigs of greenery, berries, or even flowers between the fruit. Surround the tree with tiny gift boxes wrapped in the colors of the room—we tied red Toyon berries in some of the bows.*

DECORATING WITH SILVER LEAF

potted silver topiary and silver fruit tree

GILDING FRUIT To make the gilded fruit in these decorations, you will need polystyrene fruit; two small soft-bristle paintbrushes; metallic leaf (we used silver leaf; aluminum leaf, which is also known as imitation silver leaf; and green-mint and aqua leaf); Wunda Size (for adhering metallic leaf to surfaces); and a burnishing brush of medium to soft stiffness, or a soft cotton cloth. Before you begin, wipe clean the surface of the fruit. Using one of the paintbrushes, apply a smooth, thin coat of Wunda Size to the entire fruit. Let dry for 5 minutes. Lift a piece of metallic leaf from the book (top row, left), place it carefully over the fruit, and smooth it down with the other clean paintbrush or soft cotton cloth so it covers as much of the fruit as possible; the leaf will stick to the Wunda Size. Add an additional piece of metallic leaf if the fruit is not covered completely. Let dry overnight. Using a burnishing brush or soft cotton cloth, gently remove excess leaf until the surface of the fruit is smooth (top row, right). If any spots are missing metallic leaf, apply Wunda Size and a small amount of leaf to the area, and burnish the following day. If you use real silver leaf on your fruit, you will need to coat it with a sealant like Ronan Acrylic Clear Overcoat; otherwise, it will tarnish.

MAKING THE TOPIARY You will need gilded fruit; a ceramic pot; a plastic garbage bag; hydraulic cement, like Bondex Quick Plug; a straight 15" stick 1¼" in diameter; a green 12" Styrofoam cone; a mat knife or utility knife; hot glue; scissors; toothpicks or floral picks; floral wire; fresh eucalyptus; and moss. With a knife, whittle a point on one end of the stick; set aside. To stand upright, the finished tree will need a sturdy base. Line the ceramic pot with a plastic garbage bag, then prepare the cement, following package instructions, and pour it into the pot. Insert the blunt end of the stick into the wet cement, and let set. Snip away any plastic bag that's visible. Because Styrofoam Christmas-tree cones are usually too tall and skinny for this type of project, use a mat knife or utility knife to cut and shape the cone as shown (bottom row, left); remember that the tree will become quite plump when it is covered with fruit and greenery. Center the cone over the stick, and push it down so that only two or three inches of the stick are exposed. Starting at the bottom of cone, hot glue the silver fruit to the Styrofoam (bottom row, right). The pieces of fruit should be close together, with just enough room to insert the greenery between them. With some types of greenery, you can poke the stems directly into the Styrofoam. When you can't, wire the greens onto toothpicks or floral picks, and insert them into the cone. To hide the cement, surround base of the tree with moss.

MAKING THE FRUIT TREE This fantastical tree (opposite), hung with gleaming green-mint and aqua apples and pears, is the focal point for a holiday table at Martha's East Hampton, New York, house. Embed a shapely branch in a large, heavy frog, place it in a decorative footed bowl, and surround it with green floral foam; then, lay a carpet of moss around the base. Glue silver leaves to the branches. Hang each fruit from the tree with silver ribbon tied to the fruit's stem and secured with a straight pin.

FRUIT ARRANGEMENTS

In towers, bowls, or swags,
nature's sweet gift is also a feast for the eye

What could be more glorious than a holiday table laden with fruit? Fruit is nature's bounty and an eloquent symbol of its richness. The Dutch and Flemish masters immortalized fruit, as well as flowers, in their prettiest still lifes. But it was the French, during the seventeenth and eighteenth centuries, who refined fruit centerpieces into soaring pyramids of glistening cherries and grapes; elaborate epergnes whose branches were filled with strawberries, figs, and miniature apples; or a single golden pineapple served up on a pedestal.
✳ The French built centerpieces in a variety of vessels, mixing real fruit, flowers, and leaves with ceramic fruit. Sometimes the fruit was meant to be eaten, and other times not, since some of the techniques to make a pyramid stable, like drizzling warm caramel over the arrangement or pouring water over it so it would ice, made the display purely decorative. But then a fruit centerpiece was designed less to be tasted than to dazzle and to amuse. ✳ The best fruits for creating table decorations have sturdy skins and can thrive without being refrigerated. Apples, oranges, and lemons, for example, may last several weeks; grapes stay pretty for four or five days. Combining fruit is as rich an art as arranging flowers, and just as rewarding, if you learn to appreciate fruit for its color, shape, texture, and size, as you do your favorite blooms. Be simple or be grand.

APPLE TREES *Fruit can be arranged formally, or less so. These pyramids (opposite) were inspired by eighteenth-century French designs. The large tree alternates bands of dwarf Granny Smith apples with litchi; it is flanked by trees of dwarf Gravenstein apples and princess pine. To make them, follow the technique described on page III. More relaxed displays (previous pages, left and right) are achieved by filling bowls, cordial glasses, and compotes with sugared lemons, limes, and pears.*

A single pear crowning a slender candlestick can be as eloquent as a lily in a bud vase—or a tower of plums, pears, and grapes can have the intricacy of a lavish bouquet. ✳ You can make delectable arrangements with surprising ease. Construct a tall cone of fruit simply by piercing each piece of fruit with a toothpick, then piling the fruit in circles on a Styrofoam form. Create sparkling table ornaments with a coat of spray-on adhesive and a frosting of granulated sugar. A single piece of fruit can shine, dressed with a ribbon at each place setting. ✳ For still richer arrangements, combine fruit with greenery. Sprigs of princess pine or boxwood can enliven a fruit pyramid. Red fruit will look even more vivid against bluish evergreens, like eucalyptus or white pine. Wired to a wreath or garland, apples and plums will resemble luscious Christmas-tree balls. And don't forget artificial fruit: A swag garnished with polystyrene fruit is both lightweight and long-lasting. ✳ Fruit is so vibrant it can provide a color theme for your table or the decoration of an entire dining room. To dress up a serene green-and-white dining room for the holidays, we gathered the reddest apples, pomegranates, litchi, and viburnum berries, and placed them atop the mantel and table. Fruit can also spin a mood. A spiky pineapple and the bright, sunny hues of oranges, lemons, and limes may call to mind the tropics. But what fruit does best is help you welcome the holidays, and your guests, with one of nature's sweetest, most prized gifts.

CRANBERRY PILLARS
Decorating with small fruits can be as simple as scattering cranberries around pillar candles in glass cylinders (opposite). Making a grape "pineapple" (above) will take several hours: First, hot-glue sheet moss around the base of an egg-shaped polystyrene form, then hot-glue grapes to the rest of the form. To make the tuft of leaves, put wires through stem ends of bay leaves, then secure wires with green floral tape. Hold one wired leaf, and add others around it, winding them together as you go; glue the tuft to the form. The pineapples should last up to five days.

LEMON-TASSEL SWAG
Lemons tied with ribbons are the cheerful focal point for a delicate garland made of pressed silver-tree leucodendron leaves. Frothy bunches of mimosa and eucalyptus in white ceramic urns provide more touches of yellow and silvery green. At the center of the mantel is a nineteenth-century Continental clock flanked by short pillar candles, a bouquet of paper-whites, and German glass Christmas-tree ornaments from the twenties and thirties. The nineteenth-century Spanish crystal chandelier is dressed up with sheer ribbons, seasonal berries, and sprigs of eucalyptus.

LEMON NOSEGAY *Rather than a single posy, why not offer a frosty sugared lemon at each place setting? With a gold-mesh leaf slipped beneath it, this lemon perches in a French opaline cordial glass. The pressed silver-tree leucodendron leaf and satin-edged ribbon that bind the napkin scroll echo the leafy gold border on the Wedgwood dinner plate. The underplate and butter plate are Wedgwood drabware. The celluloid-handled flatware is French. A yellow satin runner trimmed with a window-pane pattern of burnished gold-metallic ribbon covers the table.*

DECORATING A DINING ROOM

sugared lemons, lemon-tassel swag, apple pyramid, napkin scrolls, and pear place card

SUGARED LEMONS Although they're not edible, sugared lemons are long-lasting and especially easy to make. You'll need lemons; bamboo skewers; Spray-Mount, a quick-drying adhesive; granulated sugar; a spoon; a bowl; and craft paper. Insert a skewer into end of lemon. Working over craft paper, hold lemon by skewer, and coat with Spray-Mount. Sprinkle granulated sugar over lemon with spoon (far left), holding fruit over bowl to catch granules that do not adhere. Set sugared lemon on clean piece of craft paper to dry. For an informal centerpiece (left), decorate a bowl with sugared lemons and unsugared lemons tied with sheer satin-edged ribbon.

LEMON-TASSEL SWAG To make the garland on the previous page, you'll need 60 silver-tree leucodendron leaves; 3 lemons; a flower press or telephone book; white floral tape; a 6" craft needle; armature wire; 28-gauge wire; needle-nose pliers; and sheer ribbon with gold edging. In a flower press or phone book, press leaves, and let dry, about two to three days. (If using a phone book, place leaves between paper towels.) With a cool iron, smooth any curled leaves. Cut two 38" lengths of armature wire. Wrap stem end of a leaf with white floral tape, then, beginning about ½" from end of wire, wrap leaf to wire on an angle. Wrap next leaf to wire so it leans to opposite side (below left). Continue until you've secured 30 leaves. Repeat on second wire. Cut three pieces of 28-gauge wire, each 2½ times length of each lemon. Thread wire through needle, and bend a small length back. Piercing lemon at stem, push needle and wire through lemon (below center). If lemon is pierced cleanly from stem to end, no juice should be lost. Use needle-nose pliers to make loops in wire at both ends; cut excess. Tie a length of ribbon in a knot through the loop at tip of each lemon, and clip ribbon end into points. Add a longer length of ribbon, for hanging, to the loop at stem end. Repeat for the other lemons. Use pliers to make hooks at ends of

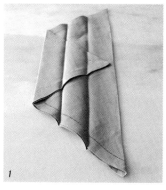
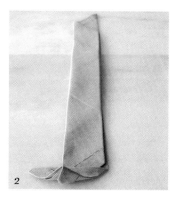

leaf garlands; cut excess wire. Attach garlands to mantel with nails or cup hooks at two ends and center. With another length of ribbon, tie three lemons together in a bow; hang from a nail or hook at center of swag.

NAPKIN SCROLLS To create these two napkin folds, start by pressing linen or cotton napkins using sizing or spray starch, and keep the iron hot. For the napkin on page 108, fold napkin in half horizontally; press along folded edge to make a crease. Then fold again to form a square; press along folded edge to make another crease. Unfold only the second crease, and place on surface with crease facing up. Roll up napkin from both sides toward crease (opposite, bottom right); tie with ribbon to hold shape. For the napkin at the place setting shown below: 1. Fold napkin in half diagonally to form a triangle; iron flat. Fold point opposite the crease to middle of crease, and iron. Fold into thirds lengthwise, ironing creases along both folds. 2. Fold napkin along creases so it's long and flat. Fold up one end of napkin one inch from the edge; hold down. 3. Begin rolling napkin up from this end, keeping tuft exposed. 4. Tuck remaining end into bottom of roll. Stand it on its base on the table, or center it on a plate.

APPLE PYRAMID Follow this basic technique for making the fruit pyramids on pages 105 and 112. For the one pictured below right, you'll need 40 to 50 dwarf Gravenstein apples; boxwood sprigs; a 12" polystyrene cone; toothpicks; and scissors. Cut off point of cone so top is flat. Poke toothpicks into bottoms of apples; insert on cone in rings, starting with largest apples at the base. Finish top with one apple. Fill in spaces by tucking short sprigs of boxwood between apples. Set pyramid atop an urn, a footed bowl, or other decorative holder.

PEAR PLACE CARD To make this quick place card (right), use pinking shears to cut a simple leaf shape from green craft paper. Write guest's name on leaf in gold ink, punch a hole in the leaf, and use narrow ribbon or seam binding to tie it to the stem of a green Seckel pear.

PEAR AND PLUM PYRAMID *The most successful fruit centerpieces pique the appetite, even when they're not meant to be plucked. Green Seckel pears, velvety purple plums, ruby-red grapes, and dark-green velvet leaves give this tower a rich, Renaissance feeling. To make it, spray-paint a polystyrene cone dark green. With toothpicks, attach the pears and plums in alternating circles. Twist floral wire to tie little stems of grapes and velvet ivy leaves with curly vines to toothpicks; insert them to fill the spaces. The pyramid rests on a hammered-silver cake stand. The double-faced satin bow adds a sumptuous touch.*

SHEER FRUIT POUCHES *Gold-mesh bags filled with pears and lady apples can be grouped on a sideboard or as a centerpiece, or used singly to mark each guest's place at the table. At the end of the evening, your guests can carry them away. To make a pouch: Cut one piece each of gold tulle and gold-metallic organza 4" wide and 8" long; pin together. With scissors, round the two corners of one of the 4" sides. Machine-stitch around the U, leaving the top open. Turn bag inside out, fill with fruit, and tie with ribbon; we slipped in a sprig of grapes and an artificial ivy leaf and vine. Snip the tops of the bags if they are too tall. These bags, which complement our pear-and-plum pyramid (above right), are grouped with an Empire-style porcelain coffee service atop a napkin the color of plums.*

PEAR AND APPLE STREAMER *This three-foot length of bay laurel, seeded eucalyptus, and artificial apples and pears makes a fitting decoration for a dining-room door or wall. For wiring to a hanging decoration, lightweight polystyrene fruit is easier to work with than real fruit, making it ideal for hanging; besides, unlike real fruit, it won't spoil before the holidays are over.*

APPLE FAVOR *Tied with sheer silver ribbon and hand-beaded leaves (see page 69), shiny red apples make tasty gifts for dinner guests, who can eat them with dessert or save them for a healthy midnight snack. Later, the leaves can be attached to gifts or ornaments. Our apple sits on an antique pressed lacy glass plate.*

DECORATING WITH REDS *Ripe red fruit and scarlet seat cushions on the Gustavian-style dining chairs transform an otherwise quiet green-and-white dining room for Christmas. On the antique brass-edged mahogany dining table, a handblown Murano glass bowl holds pears, apples, pomegranates, crab apples, and litchi nuts in countless shades of crimson; a single apple marks each place setting. A similar mix of red fruits, the papery litchi contrasting with the smooth apples, dresses up the mantel. In shimmering niches displaying a collection of creamware, tiny wrapped gifts and still more red fruit add dots of color.*

PEAR PEDESTALS *Fruit need not be sugared, pierced, or stacked to take the stage. On a mantel, pears perch on a pair of candlesticks, while wreaths of viburnum berries encircle another pair. A carpet of greenery provides contrast for the symmetrical arrangement. The eighteenth-century Venetian mirror is topped with white pine, weeping eucalyptus, and more ripe red fruit.*

SWEETS & COOKIES

*During a party, the prettiest
of all holiday decorations are often
the most delicious*

Any table laden with platters of cookies can be as joyful a symbol of Christmas as a fir tree. Indeed, the weeks between Thanksgiving and Christmas bring a deluge of sweets, and the challenge when entertaining is to make them seem special. ✳ Enchantingly displayed, almost any treats will surprise your guests. Build a centerpiece of candy canes and lollipops, and let little hands pluck away each colorful prize. Or fill a tower of cake stands with the fruit, candies, and delicious homemade cookies that seem to arrive with every visitor. And why not show off a glazed chocolate cake decorated with holly-leaf cookies on a sideboard throughout the meal? ✳ When preparing confections that will serve as centerpieces or finales, plan ahead. If you want to display a dessert during an entire meal, for example, be sure it can be left uncovered. On a dessert table, after dinner, you can plate individual servings of a gingerbread semifreddo or arrange an array of sweets. ✳ Create your treats with seasonal shapes or designs, like our almond-fudge diamonds or cinnamon snowflake wafers. Or adorn a plate of tiny cakes with flowers and trailing ribbons. Then garnish the table with beaded snowflakes or handmade paper stars. And don't forget that the simplest dessert can still bring holiday cheer. Even a fruit cake from a favorite bakery, surrounded by candles and holly leaves, can be a showstopper.

ANGEL-FOOD FOREST
Desserts can reflect the theme of the decorations of your room or table. Stacks of star-shaped angel-food cakes dusted with confectioners' sugar (opposite) look like snow-covered Christmas trees. The tablecloth has its own star motif, with handmade paper stars hanging from silver ribbons. A glazed chocolate cake (previous pages, left; recipe, page 120) is dressed with holly-leaf tuiles that echo the glittered holly leaves (see page 95) on the wreath and surrounding the candles. A red-mesh pouch of gold Jordan almonds (previous page) coordinates with the table's colors.

HOLLY-LEAF CAKE

SERVES 16

DRESSING UP A CAKE
Before it is adorned with holly
tuiles and raspberries, our
chocolate cake (below left) is
coated with a chocolate glaze.
Spread a thin layer of batter
over a stencil (below right) to
make the tuiles; a rolling pin
(bottom left) gives the still-hot
cookies their curves. Create a
vein on each tuile (bottom right)
by piping a bead of chocolate
icing down its center. The
finished cake is on page 116.

1   *tablespoon unsalted butter*
1   *cup all-purpose flour, plus more for pan*
1   *cup unsweetened cocoa powder*
¼   *teaspoon salt*
1   *teaspoon baking powder*
8   *large eggs, separated*
2   *cups sugar*
2   *teaspoons pure vanilla extract*
6   *tablespoons raspberry liqueur,*
    such as framboise
2   *recipes Shiny Chocolate Glaze, warm*
    (recipe follows)
1   *recipe Holly Tuiles (recipe follows)*
12 *raspberries, for garnish*

1. Heat oven to 350°. Butter an 11-by-17-inch baking pan. Line pan with parchment; butter and flour parchment. Set aside. Cut 5-by-10-inch rectangle out of cardboard; set aside. In medium bowl, sift together flour, cocoa, salt, and baking powder; set aside.

2. In the bowl of an electric mixer fitted with a whisk attachment, beat together egg yolks and sugar on medium-high speed until pale and thick, about 3 minutes. Scrape down the sides of bowl. Beat in the vanilla and 3 tablespoons boiling water.

3. Working in three additions, fold in dry ingredients.

4. In a separate bowl, beat egg whites until stiff but not dry; whisk one-fourth of beaten whites into the batter. Fold in remaining whites. Pour batter into prepared pan, and smooth the top with an offset spatula. Bake until cake springs back when gently pressed, 20-25 minutes. Transfer the pan to a wire rack to cool completely, about 25 minutes.

5. Turn out cake. Using a long serrated knife, trim the edges of the cooled cake. Cut cake into three 5-by-10-inch pieces. Prick all over tops of layers with a toothpick; brush with raspberry liqueur.

6. Prepare an ice bath. Transfer 2½ cups of warm chocolate glaze to a medium bowl. Place the bowl over the ice bath, and stir constantly until the glaze reaches the consistency of frosting.

7. Place one piece of cake on the reserved cardboard rectangle. Using an offset spatula, spread ¼ cup frosting over top of cake. Place a second layer of cake on top, and spread it with ¼ cup frosting. Place the third layer on top of the second, and spread 1 cup frosting over the top and sides of cake. Smooth the frosting with an offset spatula.

8. Set wire rack over baking pan. Place cake on rack. Ladle remaining warm chocolate glaze over top and sides of cake, coating evenly. Chill cake, 30 minutes.

9. To serve, place the cake on a platter. Scrape the stiffened leftover glaze from the baking pan. Fit a pastry bag with a #3 plain tip, and fill the bag with the glaze from the baking pan. Pipe small beads around the bottom of cake and around the edges of the top of cake. Pipe a row of beads three-quarters of the way down the center of each holly tuile. Decorate the cake with iced tuiles and raspberries.

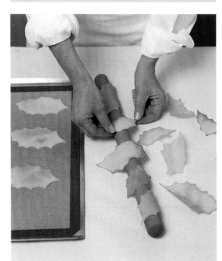

SHINY CHOCOLATE GLAZE

MAKES 2⅓ CUPS

Cooled, this recipe can be spread as a rich frosting.

- 10 ounces semisweet chocolate, chopped
- 1¼ cups heavy cream
- 4 teaspoons unsalted butter

Set a heat-proof bowl, or top of a double boiler, over a pan of simmering water. Place chocolate, heavy cream, and butter in bowl. Allow mixture to melt slowly, stirring occasionally. Remove bowl from heat. Cover, and keep warm until ready to use.

HOLLY TUILES

MAKES 26

These classic wafer cookies, named for the curved French roofing tiles that they resemble, can be made up to five days ahead, and stored in an airtight container.

- 1 large egg white
- ¼ cup superfine sugar
- ¼ cup all-purpose flour, sifted
  Pinch of salt
- 4 teaspoons unsalted butter, melted
- 2 teaspoons heavy cream
- ¼ teaspoon pure almond extract

1. Photocopy the holly-leaf templates on page 135, enlarging them to 125 percent. Find two flexible plastic lids, such as large coffee-can lids. Cut off lips of lids so the plastic lies flat. Tape a lid over each holly-leaf image. Using a utility knife, cut the leaf shapes out of plastic; set templates aside.
2. In the bowl of an electric mixer fitted with whisk attachment, combine the egg white and sugar; beat on medium speed until combined, about 30 seconds. Reduce speed to low; add the flour and salt; beat until combined. Add the melted butter, heavy cream, and almond extract; beat until combined, about 30 seconds.
3. Place a Silpat (a French nonstick baking mat; see the Guide) or parchment on a baking sheet. Place small stencil in the corner of baking sheet. Using a small offset spatula, spread a thin layer of batter over stencil. Gently lift stencil. Repeat, making ten more small leaves on baking sheet. Bake until slightly golden, about 5 minutes. Transfer pan to wire rack. Using your fingers or small offset spatula, quickly drape hot cookies over rolling pin to cool.
4. Repeat step four, using the large holly stencil to make sixteen large tuiles.

CANDY-CANE "FOUNTAIN" *This colorful centerpiece makes pure holiday magic. Begin by stacking a clear-glass vase and a clear-glass compote. Fill the vase with candy canes and the compote with mints. Then insert more candy canes around the sides of the compote, among the mints. If you don't have a compote or a vase that's right, experiment with what you have, like cake stands, goblets, or drinking glasses. Try scattering hard candies, like confetti, on a cake stand.*

ANGEL-FOOD TREES

SERVES 6

The cake may be made up to two days ahead. Store tightly wrapped in plastic wrap; cut just before serving.

- 1 tablespoon unsalted butter, for pan
- 1 cup sifted cake flour (not self-rising), plus more for pan
- 1½ cups superfine sugar
- 1¾ cups (about 14 large) egg whites, room temperature
- ½ teaspoon salt
- 1½ teaspoons cream of tartar
- 1 teaspoon pure vanilla extract
- 1 teaspoon pure almond extract
- 1 cup heavy cream
- 2 tablespoons confectioners' sugar, plus 3 tablespoons for dusting
- 1 recipe Raspberry Coulis (recipe below)
- 1 cup raspberries

1. Heat oven to 350°. Butter an 11-by-17-inch baking pan, and line with parchment. Butter and flour parchment; set aside. In a medium bowl, whisk together flour and ¾ cup superfine sugar; set aside.
2. In bowl of electric mixer fitted with whisk attachment, beat egg whites with 1 tablespoon warm water on low speed until foamy, about 3 minutes. Add salt, cream of tartar, and vanilla and almond extracts; beat on medium-high speed until soft peaks form. Sprinkle in remaining ¾ cup superfine sugar, 1 tablespoon at a time, beating on high speed until stiff but not dry.
3. Transfer the batter to a large bowl. In four additions, sift the flour mixture over the egg-white mixture, folding in after each addition.
4. Fill a large pastry bag with the batter. Evenly pipe the batter in rows into the prepared pan, and lightly smooth the top with a large offset spatula.
5. Bake cake until the top is golden brown and springs back when pressed, about 20 minutes. Transfer the pan to a wire rack to cool.
6. Using a graduated set of Ateco plain star cookie cutters (see the Guide), cut out six of the following: 4-inch, 3¼-inch, 2½-inch, and 1¼-inch stars. Using back of a pastry tip, cut out six ¾-inch circles. Sift 3 tablespoons confectioners' sugar over tops of shapes.
7. Place the six largest stars on six dessert plates. Stack the remaining stars, going from largest to smallest, forming Christmas-tree shapes. Top each Christmas tree with a small cake circle. Cover the trees with plastic wrap until ready to serve.

8. To serve, whisk heavy cream and 2 tablespoons confectioners' sugar until stiff in a chilled medium bowl. Dollop whipped cream on each cake; garnish with a spoonful of the coulis and a few raspberries.

RASPBERRY COULIS

MAKES 1 CUP

If you do not own a food processor, run the cooked berries through a fine food mill.

- 1 pint fresh raspberries
- 3 tablespoons sugar

1. Place raspberries, sugar, and 2 tablespoons water in small heavy-bottomed saucepan. Bring to simmer over medium-high heat. Reduce heat to medium, and cook, stirring occasionally, until raspberries are saucy and have broken down, about 6 minutes.
2. Transfer sauce to a food processor; process for 1 minute. Place fine sieve over bowl. Pass raspberries through sieve, discarding seeds. Store coulis, refrigerated, in airtight container until ready to use.

SHINY CHOCOLATE PETITS FOURS

MAKES 35

These bite-size cakes can be stored, uncovered, for up to two days in the refrigerator.

- ½ cup sugar
- ⅔ cup strong brewed coffee
- 1 recipe Chocolate Génoise (recipe on page 124)
- 3 recipes Shiny Chocolate Glaze, warm (recipe on page 121)
- 140 No. 1-size gold dragées

1. Place sugar and coffee in small saucepan. Bring to a boil over medium heat, stirring continuously. Remove from heat when sugar has dissolved. Let cool.
2. Turn génoise out onto a cutting board, and peel off paper. Trim ½ inch off edges with a serrated knife. Cut génoise in half, making two 8-by-10-inch pieces. Brush the tops generously with cooled syrup.
3. Prepare an ice bath. Transfer ¾ cup of chocolate glaze in a medium bowl placed over an ice bath. Whisk glaze until fluffy, lightened, and thick. Using an offset spatula, evenly spread whipped glaze over one piece of génoise. Place second piece of génoise squarely on top of first.
4. Using a ruler and a serrated knife, cut stacked

RED-ROSE TOWER
Stacked pressed-glass cake stands (opposite) are the base for an enticing centerpiece arrayed with shiny, gold-studded chocolate petits fours, roses in antique cranberry-colored pony glasses, and a cascade of mesh ribbons. Because it's open and airy, this arrangement allows guests to see across the table. The napkins provide a backdrop of deep red for the Leeds pottery transferware plates.

GOLD PIECES *To dress up our glazed chocolate-génoise petits fours for the holiday centerpiece on the previous page, we dotted each one with four gold dragées. The dragées will sit firmly in place atop the bite-size cakes if you add them after the shiny chocolate glaze has set. To keep from smudging the icing, try using tweezers to place each dragée.*

cake into 1¼-inch squares. Set two wire racks over two baking pans. Arrange cake squares on racks, spacing them 1½ inches apart.

5. Generously ladle warm glaze over squares, covering tops and sides. Refrigerate pans for 10 minutes.

6. Place four dragées in the center of each petit four. Using a small offset spatula, transfer petits fours to a cake stand or serving platter.

CHOCOLATE GÉNOISE

MAKES ONE 11-BY-17-INCH CAKE

   5   *tablespoons unsalted butter, melted, plus more for pan*

  ²/₃ *cup sifted cake flour (not self-rising)*

  ¹/₃ *cup sifted cocoa powder, plus more for dusting pan*

       Pinch of baking soda

   6   *large eggs*

  ³/₄ *cup sugar*

   2   *teaspoons pure vanilla extract*

1. Heat oven to 350°. Butter an 11-by-17-inch baking pan. Line with parchment; butter and powder paper; set aside. In a medium bowl, sift together the flour, cocoa, and baking soda; set aside.

2. In the bowl of an electric mixer, whisk together eggs, sugar, and vanilla. Set over pan of simmering water; whisk until the mixture is warm and the sugar has dissolved. Remove from heat, and transfer to mixer. Using a whisk attachment, beat on high speed until the mixture is thick, pale, and tripled in bulk, about 6 minutes.

3. In three additions, sift reserved flour mixture over egg mixture, folding in after each addition. While folding in last addition, pour in the melted butter; fold in thoroughly.

4. Transfer to pan; smooth batter with offset spatula. Tap pan on counter to remove air bubbles. Bake until cake springs back when touched in center, 15 to 20 minutes. Let pan cool on wire rack. Turn out cake; cover with plastic wrap until ready to use.

GINGERBREAD SEMIFREDDO

SERVES 10 TO 12

To make this half-frozen cake, you'll need full recipes of the following: Gingerbread Génoise, Semifreddo Mixture, Cranberry Coulis, Sugared Cranberries and Rosemary, as well as ³/₄ cup Calvados Soaking Syrup (all recipes given below). Make the semifreddo mixture first, and freeze. To assemble, make sure the génoise is completely cool, and follow these instructions:

1. Unroll génoise; brush generously with Calvados soaking syrup. Quickly spread semifreddo mixture over surface to within one inch of edges. Roll cake into jelly-roll shape; wrap with a towel to cover. Freeze until hard, about 5 hours or overnight.

2. To serve, temper slightly in refrigerator, about 15 minutes, and slice. Put coulis on plate first, then place slice on top; use 2 or 3 sugared cranberries and a sprig of sugared rosemary for garnish.

GINGERBREAD GÉNOISE

MAKES ONE 11-BY-17-INCH CAKE

   6   *tablespoons unsalted butter, melted, plus more for pan*

 1¼ *cups all-purpose flour, plus more for pan*

  ½ *cup confectioners' sugar*

 1½ *teaspoons ground ginger*

 1½ *teaspoons ground cinnamon*

  ¼ *teaspoon ground cloves*

  ¼ *teaspoon ground nutmeg*

   1   *cup packed dark-brown sugar*

   6   *large eggs*

   1   *tablespoon unsulfured molasses*

1. Heat oven to 350°. Butter 11-by-17-inch jelly-roll pan; line with parchment. Butter and flour parchment; set aside. Place a clean, smooth kitchen towel on a clean surface; sift confectioners' sugar evenly over towel. In medium bowl, whisk together flour, ginger, cinnamon, cloves, and nutmeg; set aside.

2. Set the bowl of an electric mixer over, but not touching, a pan of simmering water. Combine brown sugar and eggs in the bowl; whisk until a candy thermometer registers 110° (warm to the touch), about 2 minutes.

3. Beat egg mixture on high until pale and thick, 6 to 8 minutes. Using a rubber spatula, transfer mixture to large bowl. In three additions, add flour mixture, folding in after each. In small bowl, combine melted butter and molasses; add to batter in steady stream while folding in last flour addition. Pour batter into prepared pan; smooth top with an offset spatula.

4. Bake until cake is springy to the touch and golden brown, about 14 minutes. Transfer to wire rack for 5

minutes. Carefully turn out cake over towel. Place shorter end toward you. Pick up edge of towel; begin rolling cake. As you roll, incorporate towel; continue rolling into a log. Transfer to wire rack to cool

CALVADOS SOAKING SYRUP

MAKES 1½ CUPS

1   cup sugar
5   tablespoons Calvados or brandy

In a saucepan set over medium-high heat, combine the sugar and 1 cup water. Cook, stirring, until the sugar has dissolved, 4 to 5 minutes. Remove from heat; set aside to cool. Stir in the Calvados. Store, refrigerated, in an airtight container.

SEMIFREDDO MIXTURE

SERVES 10 TO 12

6   large egg yolks
⅓   cup sugar
⅓   cup Calvados or brandy
2   cups heavy cream

1. In bowl of an electric mixer, beat egg yolks until pale and thick. Gradually add sugar; beat until fluffy. Slowly add Calvados, and beat to combine.
2. Hold bowl over, but not touching, pan of simmering water. Whisk until shiny and thick, about 8 minutes. Return to mixer; beat on medium speed until cool, about 10 minutes.
3. In a chilled bowl, whip cream until soft peaks form. Add one-fourth of the whipped cream to egg mixture; whisk to combine. Fold in remaining whipped cream. Transfer to a 9-by-13-inch metal pan. Cover, and freeze, until hardened, 3 to 4 hours. Then use mixture to fill cake.

CRANBERRY COULIS

MAKES 1⅔ CUPS

8   ounces fresh or frozen cranberries
6   tablespoons sugar
2   one-by-three-inch slices orange peel
1   stick cinnamon

1. In small saucepan, combine all ingredients with 1½ cups water; bring to boil. Reduce heat to medium low; cook until cranberries have burst, 8 to 10 minutes. Remove and discard peel and cinnamon.
2. Pass mixture through a food mill, and then through a fine sieve; remove all seeds. Let cool. Store refrigerated in an airtight container.

SUGARED CRANBERRIES
AND ROSEMARY

MAKES ½ CUP

¾   cup Calvados Soaking Syrup
       (recipe above)
½   teaspoon sugar
½   cup fresh cranberries
12 sprigs rosemary

1. Line two baking sheets with parchment; set aside. Pour soaking syrup into a medium bowl; place the sugar in a large one.
2. Insert wooden toothpick into a cranberry. Dip into syrup, tap off excess, and roll in sugar. Set on parchment. Repeat with remaining cranberries.
3. Sugar rosemary sprigs as in step two, holding sprigs by stems. Store in an airtight container.

FROSTY GINGERBREAD
This semifreddo—Italian for "half cold"—makes a surprising alternative to a traditional bûche de Noël. Prepare the gingerbread génoise and the creamy filling the day before the dessert is to be eaten, roll them together, then freeze. Serve each slice atop cranberry coulis and garnished with sugared cranberries and sprigs of sugared rosemary.

*To make our ribbon cookies,
spread batter (below left) over
a Silpat mat (a French nonstick
baking mat, see the Guide) with
an offset spatula. After baking,
cut cookie into strips (below
right), and lay strips across an
oven rack so they harden in
waves. To create the design on
our cinnamon snowflake
wafers, sift confectioners' sugar
over the rolled dough before
baking (bottom left), using a
homemade paper snowflake as
a stencil. Diamonds of almond
fudge layered with edible
silver leaf (bottom right) can
be arranged into stars.*

LACY RIBBON COOKIES

MAKES 32

*A cool, clean oven rack, set over a baking sheet, is the
perfect tool for shaping these cookies.*

> 1 cup (2 sticks) plus 5 tablespoons unsalted
> butter, room temperature
> 2¼ cups confectioners' sugar
> ¼ cup light corn syrup
> 1¼ cups bread flour

1. Remove an oven rack from your oven, and set
over an 11-by-17-inch baking sheet on a work
surface. Heat oven to 350°.

2. In the bowl of an electric mixer fitted with the
paddle attachment, cream the butter and sugar on
medium speed until fluffy. With the mixer running,
add the corn syrup. Turn speed to low, and add the
flour. Mix until incorporated.

3. Line an 11-by-17-inch baking pan with a Silpat
(a French nonstick baking mat; see the Guide).
Transfer ¾ cup batter onto the Silpat; using an offset spatula, spread the batter evenly over mat.
Bake until golden brown and lacy, about 10 minutes, rotating once for even baking. Transfer to a
heat-proof surface to cool for 10 seconds.

4. Using a pastry wheel, cut the single, large
cookie into 1½-by-11-inch strips. Using your
fingers or an offset spatula, transfer the strips to
the oven rack. Use your fingers to drape each strip
over the rack, making it into a curvy ribbon.
Repeat the process with the remaining cookie
strips. If the strips become too hard to bend,
return them to the oven for 1 minute to resoften.

5. Repeat steps three and four with the remaining
batter. The cookies can be stored in an airtight container for up to 1 week.

SNOWFLAKE WAFERS

MAKES 8 SIX-INCH WAFERS

*Fold and cut your own paper snowflakes to use as sten-
cils for these delicate wafers.*

> 1 cup all-purpose flour, plus more for dusting
> ½ teaspoon salt
> 2 tablespoons granulated sugar
> ½ teaspoon ground cinnamon
> 3 tablespoons unsalted butter, cut
> into 6 pieces
> ⅓ cup milk
> 6 tablespoons confectioners' sugar

1. Heat oven to 325°. Line four baking pans with
parchment paper; set aside. Sprinkle work surface
generously with flour.

2. In the bowl of a food processor, pulse together
flour, salt, granulated sugar, and cinnamon. Add
butter, and pulse until mixture resembles coarse
meal. With machine running, gradually add the
milk; process until dough comes together.

3. Transfer dough to floured work surface. Cut into
eight equal pieces, and form each piece into a ball.
Roll out balls into 7-inch disks, and place two on
each baking pan. Place a snowflake over a disk.

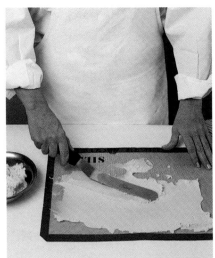

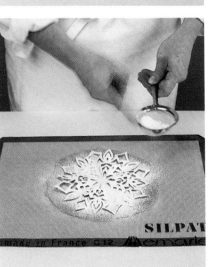

Sift 1 tablespoon confectioners' sugar over stencil. Gently lift stencil. Repeat with remaining disks.

4. Bake until lightly browned, about 18 minutes. Let cool. Store in airtight container for up to 5 days.

SILVER-LEAFED ALMOND FUDGE
MAKES ABOUT 3 DOZEN PIECES

Edible silver leaf is sometimes used in decorating cakes; look for it at specialty baking-supply stores.

- 1 *cup heavy cream*
- 1 *cup milk*
- 3/4 *cup sugar*
- 1/2 *teaspoon pure almond extract*
- 2 *cups blanched almond flour (see the Guide)*
- 1/2 *teaspoon salt*
- 4 *four-inch pieces edible silver leaf (see the Guide)*

1. Line an 8-inch-square baking pan with parchment paper, and set aside.

2. Place cream and milk in a medium saucepan set over medium-high heat. Bring to a boil, and cook, uncovered, until thick enough to coat the back of a spoon, about 15 minutes. Add sugar and almond extract; cook, stirring, until sugar has dissolved, about 2 minutes. While stirring, add the almond flour and salt. Reduce heat to medium, and continue stirring until mixture is very stiff and pulls away from the sides of the pan, about 3 minutes.

3. Transfer mixture to prepared pan; use a rubber spatula to smooth the top. Let cool 5 minutes.

4. Peel top piece of paper off packet of silver leaf, revealing a single sheet of leaf. Place booklet, silver leaf facing down, on fudge, lining up booklet's corner with the corner of fudge. Press on back of booklet to affix silver leaf to fudge. Peel off booklet. Repeat process three times, covering each quadrant of the fudge. Let the fudge cool 30 minutes.

5. Cut fudge in 1-inch-wide slices diagonally; then cut 1-inch-wide slices vertically, creating diamond shapes. With an offset spatula, transfer the fudge to an airtight container. Store, refrigerated, until ready to serve.

FRUIT TOWER *Making an edible centerpiece can be as simple as stacking several compotes (above) and filling them with fresh and dried fruit. Tuck in sprigs of boxwood to fill the spaces. We topped this tower with a cup of dark-chocolate twigs and a sprig of holly.*

GOLDEN SIDEBOARD *A dessert table (following pages) holds all that is needed after a special late-night supper: glistening diamonds of almond fudge, crisp snowflake wafers, buttery ribbon cookies, winter fruit, and a carafe of dessert wine. The fudge is arranged on a square of inexpensive raw silk whose edges have been pulled by hand to create a fringed border. Venetian-glass and transferware compotes hold the oversize wafers and cookies.*

TEMPLATES

Use these templates for projects in the Fabrics & Trimmings, Gingerbread, and Sweets & Cookies chapters. Photocopy the templates, enlarging or reducing as suggested. For the holly-leaf tuile stencils, you'll need a flat, flexible piece of plastic, like the lid from a coffee can; to make the other templates, you'll need craft paper or thin cardboard.

FELT MINI STOCKING AND SATIN ORNAMENT *Use the stocking template (far left) to make the felt mini stockings on pages 54 and 55. Photocopy the template, enlarging it to 125 percent or the size you desire. To make the satin ornaments on page 53, use the template at left: For 2" balls, reduce template to 90 percent on a photocopier; for 3" balls, enlarge template to 125 percent. To make over-size ornaments, like the kissing ball on page 48, enlarge template on a photocopier to fit the ball, pole to pole.*

FANCY STOCKING

To make the stockings on pages 51 and 52, double the size of this template on a photocopier, or enlarge the template to whatever size you wish. To make the lattice-pattern stocking, trace grid onto tracing paper, and follow the instructions on page 52. To make a diagonally striped stocking, trace only one set of parallel lines. You can also use the lines of the grid to plot evenly spaced polka dots.

GINGERBREAD
ORNAMENTS *Use these
templates to shape and decorate
the cookies on pages 70 and
71 and on pages 78 and 79. On
a photocopier, enlarge the
templates to 125 percent. Trace
them onto thin cardboard,
and cut them out. Using the
templates, cut the cookies
from the chilled dough; before
baking, remember to make
holes for hanging. Decorate
cookies following the patterns
shown here, or create your
own designs. Apply a smooth
layer of floodwork icing before
piping the designs in another
color, or apply designs directly
to cookie, letting the gingerbread itself be the background.*

GOTHIC COTTAGE

To make the three-sided ginger-bread-house facade shown on pages 72, 82, and 83, use templates opposite and to the right. Our house is 14³/₄" tall at the peak of the roof; for this size, enlarge the templates to 165 percent on a photocopier, then trace the templates onto lightweight cardboard. Cut out the four windowpanes on each of the six windows of the template, and cut out panes from dough before baking front of house. Refer to designs on templates when decorating the house with royal icing and flocking with sanding sugar.

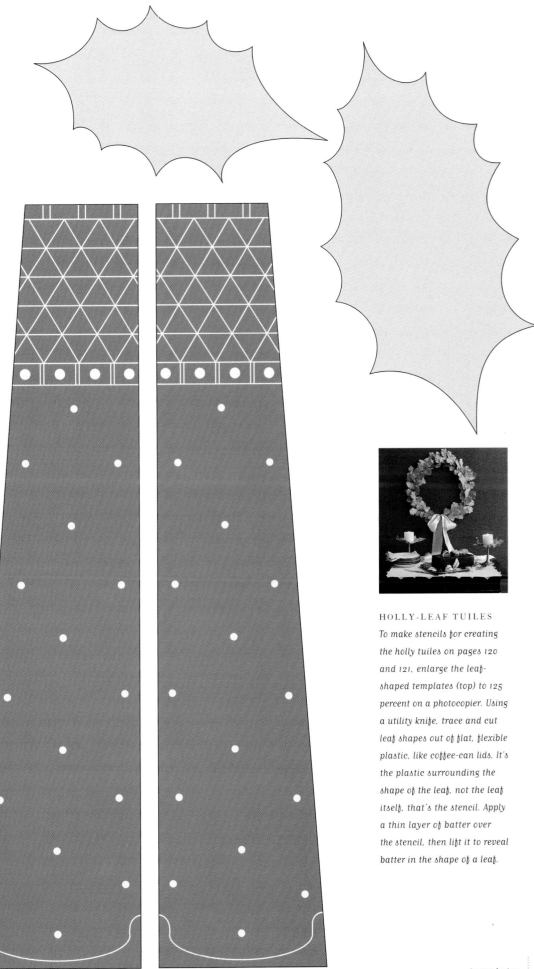

HOLLY-LEAF TUILES

To make stencils for creating the holly tuiles on pages 120 and 121, enlarge the leaf-shaped templates (top) to 125 percent on a photocopier. Using a utility knife, trace and cut leaf shapes out of flat, flexible plastic, like coffee-can lids. It's the plastic surrounding the shape of the leaf, not the leaf itself, that's the stencil. Apply a thin layer of batter over the stencil, then lift it to reveal batter in the shape of a leaf.

THE GUIDE

Items pictured but not listed are from private collections. Addresses and telephone numbers of sources may change prior to or following publication, as may price and availability of any item.

COVER

SWEATER by Loro Piana. PANTS by Prada. TAFFETA GINGHAM RIBBON from Hyman Hendler & Sons, 67 West 38th Street, New York, NY 10018; 212-840-8393. Minimum order $75. VINTAGE TOILE SCREEN from John Rosselli, Ltd., 255 East 72nd Street, New York, NY 10021; 212-737-2252. To the trade only. CASHMERE WRAP (ACW002), $359, and FEATHER CHRISTMAS TREE from Martha By Mail, 800-950-7130. RUG from ABC Carpet & Home, 888 Broadway, New York, NY 10003; 212-473-3000. LINEN-UPHOLSTERED CHAIR, $3,950, and COFFEE TABLE, $1,110, from Gomez Associates, 504 East 74th Street, 3rd Floor, New York, NY 10021; 212-288-6856. MARTHA STEWART EVERYDAY COLORS PAINT in "American Green" (D11) on wall, available at Kmart, 800-866-0086 for store locations; and Sears mall stores, 800-972-4687 for locations.

SNOWMEN

page 13

STRIPED WOOL HAT from J. Crew; 800-562-0258 to order. Free catalog. ARTIFICIAL GRAPES, 99¢ to $6.70 per bunch, from Bill's Flower Market, 816 Sixth Avenue, New York, NY 10001; 212-889-8154.

page 16

SNOWBALLER from FAO Schwarz, 767 Fifth Avenue, New York, NY 10153; 212-644-9400.

FRONT DOORS

pages 18 to 29

RIBBONS from: Hyman Hendler & Sons, 67 West 38th Street, New York, NY 10018; 212-840-8393. Minimum order $75. Tinsel Trading Co., 47 West 38th Street, New York, NY 10018; 212-730-1030. GREENERY from: Fischer & Page, 134 West 28th Street, New York, NY 10001; 212-645-4106. US Evergreen, 805 Sixth Avenue, New York, NY 10001; 212-741-5300. MAGNOLIA GARLANDS, $12 per foot, from US Evergreen, see above. SINGLE-WIRE WREATH FORMS from Oregon Wire Products, 13030 NE Whitaker Way, Portland, OR 97220; or

write P.O. Box 20279, Portland, OR 97294; 800-458-8344. HOLIDAY LIGHTS from Just Bulbs, 936 Broadway, New York, NY 10010; 212-228-7820.

GARLANDS & BLOSSOMS

pages 30 to 43

ASSORTED RIBBONS from: Hyman Hendler & Sons, 67 West 38th Street, New York, NY 10018; 212-840-8393. Minimum order $75. Tinsel Trading Co., 47 West 38th Street, New York, NY 10018; 212-730-1030. GREENERY from: Fischer & Page, 134 West 28th Street, New York, NY 10001; 212-645-4106. US Evergreen, 805 Sixth Avenue, New York, NY 10001; 212-741-5300. Joe Makrancy's Floral & Garden Shop, 966 Kuser Road, Trenton, NJ 08619; 609-587-2543. Green Valley Growers, 10450 Cherry Ridge Road, Sebastopol, CA 95472; 707-823-5583. WIRED SILVER BALLS, DULLING SPRAY, and DRIED POMEGRANATES available at crafts and floral-supply stores nationwide.

page 30

CANED SETTEE from Theron Ware, Works of Art, 548 Warren Street, Hudson, NY 12534; 518-828-9744. ENGLISH BOXWOOD from Fischer & Page, see above.

page 31

RED GLASS TUMBLERS from L. Becker Flowers, 217 East 83rd Street, New York, NY 10028; 212-439-6001.

page 33

LOUIS XVI GILT-WOOD BAROMETER WITH PEN-AND-INK DRAWING, $9,500, and ANTIQUE DEMILUNE TABLE from Malmaison Antiques, 253 East 74th Street, New York, NY 10021; 212-288-7569. EMBOSSED WRAPPING PAPER SET (CMM004), $28, from Martha By Mail, 800-950-7130.

page 34

TWO-DRAWER STAND from Benjamin Wilson Antiques, 513 Warren Street, Hudson, NY 12534;

518-822-0866. NINETEENTH-CENTURY VENETIAN VASE from Theron Ware, Works of Art, see above.

page 35

GLAZED CERAMIC FLOWER POTS from Takashimaya, 693 Fifth Avenue, New York, NY 10022; 212-350-0100 or 800-753-2038.

page 36

ENGLISH REGENCY SOFA from Botanicus Antiques, Inc., 446 Warren Street, Hudson, NY 12534; 518-828-0866.

page 37

WOODEN CRANBERRY BEADS (#02047) from Midwest of Cannon Falls; 800-377-3335 for nearest retailer. DEMILUNE TABLE from Evergreen Antiques, 1249 Third Avenue, New York, NY 10021; 212-744-5664.

page 42

GREEN PILLAR CANDLES, $7.50 to $25, from Susan Schadt, Inc., 990 Highland Drive, Suite 104B, Solana Beach, CA 92075; 619-793-0400 for store information. ANTIQUE GREEN-GLASS BOWL from James II Galleries, Ltd., 11 East 57th Street, 4th Floor, New York, NY 10022; 212-355-7040.

page 43

ANTIQUE REGENCY PAINTED DINING CHAIRS from Theron Ware, Works of Art, see above.

FABRICS & TRIMMINGS

pages 46 and 47

2" and 3" STYROFOAM BALLS available at crafts stores nationwide. 54"-WIDE PALE-GREEN SILK TAFFETA, $39.95 per yard, and 48"-WIDE RED SILK-FACED SATIN, $36.95 per yard, from B&J Fabrics, 263 West 40th Street, New York, NY 10018; 212-354-8150. BABY-BLUE POLYESTER VELVET, $14.95 per yard, from Elegant Fabrics, 240 West 40th Street, New York, NY 10018; 212-302-4984. 6" PALE-BLUE RAYON TAFFETA RIBBON, $12.50 per yard, from Hyman Hendler & Sons, 67 West 38th Street, New York, NY 10018; 212-840-8393. Minimum order $75. ASSORTED SILVER RIBBON, PLATINUM WATCH STRAPPING, $6 to $7.50 per yard, SILVER BULLION TWIST, $3 per yard, SILVER BALLS, $2.50 each, SILVER TASSELS, $7 and up, SILVER RICKRACK, $2.50 per yard, and SILVER TWINE, $1.50 and up, from Tinsel Trading Co., 47 West 38th Street, New York, NY 10018; 212-730-1030. RED-AND-WHITE

PLAID RIBBON, $3.98 per yard, from M&J Trimming, 1008 Sixth Avenue, New York, NY 10018; 212-391-9072. PEARL-HEAD PINS available at sewing, crafts, and floral-supply stores nationwide.

page 48

METALLIC RIBBON from Tinsel Trading Co., see above. 8" STYROFOAM BALL, $17.50, from Kervar, Inc., 119 West 28th Street, New York, NY 10001; 212-564-2525. 54"-WIDE PALE-GREEN SILK TAFFETA, $39.95 per yard, from B&J Fabrics, see above. KISSING BALL KIT available in other colors from Martha By Mail, 800-950-7130. CEDAR AND EUCALYPTUS GARLAND, $6 per foot, from US Evergreen, 805 Sixth Avenue, New York, NY 10001; 212-741-5300.

page 51

56"-WIDE TURQUOISE SILK SATIN, $82.95 per yard, 48"-WIDE RED SILK-FACED SATIN, $36.95 per yard, 45"-WIDE PALE-GREEN SILK SHANTUNG, $15.95 per yard, and 45"-WIDE RED POLYESTER VELVET, $21.95 per yard, from B&J Fabrics, see above. BABY-BLUE POLYESTER VELVET, $14.95 per yard, from Elegant Fabrics, see above. ASSORTED SATIN RIBBONS, 39¢ and up per yard, and 6MM FAUX PEARLS, $5.98 per strand, from M&J Trimming, see above. CEDAR AND WHITE-PINE GARLAND, $6 per foot, from US Evergreen, see above. CIRCA 1860 ENGLISH MIRROR IN SILVER-LEAFED FRAME, $2,400, from Gomez Associates, 504 East 74th Street, 3rd Floor, New York, NY 10021; 212-288-6856.

page 54

SAGE, LEAF, and SHELL WOOL FELT, $2.95 per 9"-by-12" sheet, from Magic Cabin Dolls; 888-623-6557. RED-AND-WHITE PLAID RIBBON, $3.98 per yard, GINGHAM and GROSGRAIN RIBBONS, $1.98 to $3.98 per yard, from M&J Trimming, see above. WIRE-RIMMED TAGS available at stationery stores nationwide. HOTEL-SILVER RECTANGULAR TRAY, $450, HOTEL-SILVER TOAST RACK, $425, and 8" HOTEL-SILVER BOWL, $545, from Bergdorf Goodman, 754 Fifth Avenue, New York, NY 10019; 212-753-7300 or 800-218-4918.

page 56

3" TO 6" SATIN RIBBONS, $6.50 to $15 per yard, and GROSGRAIN RIBBONS, $7.50 to $15 per yard, from Hyman Hendler & Sons, see above. VINTAGE TAGS, 50¢ each, from Bell'occhio, 8 Brady Street, San Francisco, CA 94103; 415-864-4048.

page 57

GALVANIZED BUCKET, $14, from IKEA; 410-931-8940 for East Coast locations and mail order, 626-912-1119 for West Coast locations and mail order.

BEADS

pages 58 to 69

BEAD PROJECT KIT (CBP001), $48, from Martha By Mail, 800-950-7130. ASSORTED BEADS from: Meyer Imports, 25 West 37th Street, New York, NY 10018; 212-391-3830. $50 minimum order; catalog $7.50. Elliot, Greene & Co., Inc., 37 West 37th Street, New York, NY 10018; 212-391-9075. $25 minimum order; catalog $5. Ornamental Resources, P.O. Box 3010-MS, 1427 Miner Street, Idaho Springs, CO 80452; 800-876-6762. Catalog $15. General Bead, 317 National City Boulevard, National City, CA 91950; 619-336-0100. Catalog $4. Bead Lovers' Catalog, $3, from the Beadbox, P.O. Box 6035, Scottsdale, AZ 85261-6035; 800-232-3269. ASSORTED WIRES from: Gampel Supply, 11 West 37th Street, New York, NY 10018; 212-398-9222. Free catalog. Metalliferous, 34 West 46th Street, New York, NY 10036; 212-944-0909. Catalog $7.50.

page 58

1½" and 2" POLYSTYRENE BALLS available at crafts stores nationwide. 24- AND 28-GAUGE TINNED COPPER WIRE, $4.50 per ¼-pound spool, available from Gampel Supply, see above. SILVER TWINE, $1.50 per yard, from Tinsel Trading Co., 47 West 38th Street, New York, NY 10018; 212-730-1030.

page 59

HEPPLEWHITE SHIELD-BACKED CHAIR from Gomez Associates, 504 East 74th Street, 3rd Floor, New York, NY 10021; 212-288-6856. TOYON-BERRY WREATH from Green Valley Growers, 10450 Cherry Ridge Road, Sebastopol, CA 95472; 707-823-5583. EMBOSSED WRAPPING PAPER SET (CMM004), $28, from Martha By Mail, 800-950-7130.

page 60

PICTURE FRAME from Skyframe, 96 Spring Street, New York, NY 10012; 212-925-7856.

page 63

BEADED-SNOWFLAKE KIT (CBS001), $48, from Martha By Mail, 800-950-7130. SILVER TWINE, $1.50 per yard, from Tinsel Trading Co., see above.

page 64

4-MM GREEN SILK EMBROIDERY RIBBON, $8 for 25 yards, from Tinsel Trading Co., see above. TURQUOISE FLINT PAPER, $1 per sheet, from New York Central Art Supply, 62 Third Avenue, New York, NY 10003; 212-473-7705 or 800-950-6111. Free catalog. PEPPERMINT PILLOWS, $7.50 per pound, from Hammond's Candies, 2550 West 29th Avenue, Denver, CO 80211; 888-226-3999. Free catalog.

page 65

SIDE CUTTERS, $7.50, and ROUND- and FLAT-NOSED PLIERS, $6.50 each, from Metalliferous, see above. BEADED-SNOWFLAKE KIT (CBS001), $48, from Martha By Mail, 800-950-7130.

page 66

GUM-PASTE BELL MOLD (BM161), $9.99, from New York Cake & Baking Distributors, 56 West 22nd Street, New York, NY 10010; 212-675-2253 or 800-942-2539. 2-MM BLUE and 4-MM GREEN SILK EMBROIDERY RIBBON, $8 for 25 yards, and ¼" BRAIDED SILVER RIBBON, $2.50 per yard, from Tinsel Trading Co., see above. 30- AND 34-GAUGE TINNED COPPER WIRE, $2.50 to $4.50, from Gampel Supply, see above.

page 68

26-GAUGE TINNED COPPER WIRE, $4.50 per ¼-pound spool, from Gampel Supply, see above. 19-GAUGE NICKEL SILVER WIRE, $1.75 per foot, from Metalliferous, see above. 3-foot minimum, or 1-pound spool for $15.35. 1" SILVER-MESH RIBBON, $4 per yard, from Tinsel Trading Co., see above.

GINGERBREAD

pages 70 and 71

LIGHT-BLUE CANDLES, $3 to $4 for box of 20, and TREE CLIPS, $9 for set of 10, from The Candle Shop, 118 Christopher Street, New York, NY 10014; 212-989-0148 or 888-823-4823. SILVER CORD, 39¢ to $3.98 per yard, from M&J Trimming, 1008 Sixth Avenue, New York, NY 10018; 212-391-9072.

page 72

TAFFETA RIBBON from Hyman Hendler & Sons, 67 West 38th Street, New York, NY 10018; 212-840-8393. Minimum order $75. GIANT REINDEER AND SNOW CRYSTAL COOKIE CUTTER SET (KMB008), $45, from Martha By Mail, 800-950-7130.

page 75

MOON AND STAR COOKIE CUTTER SET (KMB001), $45, NOAH'S ARK COOKIE CUTTER SET (CNA001) with nine copper animal cutters and template for ark, $78, and ENAMELWARE BUCKET (GWB001), 11" x 11½", $19, from Martha By Mail, 800-950-7130. EUCALYPTUS, SEEDED EUCALYPTUS, ACACIA BAILEYANA, AND SANTOLINA GARLAND from Green Valley Growers, 10450 Cherry Ridge Road, Sebastopol, CA 95472; 707-823-5583.

page 76

8" TO 12" PASTRY BAGS, $2.49 to $4.99, 12" DISPOSABLE PASTRY BAGS, $1.99 for 10, ICING TIPS, 99¢ to $2.49, SANDING SUGAR, $1.99 for 4 ounces, ICING DYE, $1.39 to $1.99 for 1 ounce, and PETAL DUST, $3 for 2 to 4 grams, from New York Cake & Baking Distributors, 56 West 22nd Street, New York, NY 10010; 800-942-2539 or 212-675-2253. SILPAT BAKING MATS, $18 for 11¼" by 16½" (KSP002), $27 for 16½" by 24¼" (KSP001), from Martha By Mail, 800-950-7130. MARTHA'S BLUE SHIRT AND TAN JODHPURS from Ralph Lauren Collection, Polo Ralph Lauren, 867 Madison Avenue, New York, NY 10021; 212-606-2100 for store locations. GREEN CASHMERE SWEATER, by Lorena Antoniazzi, available at Barneys New York; 212-826-8900 for store locations. LARA'S SHIRT AND NAVY CORDUROY OVERALLS from Gap Kids; 800-333-7899 for store locations.

page 77

NOAH'S ARK COOKIE CUTTER SET (CNA001) with nine copper animal cutters (penguin not included) and template for ark, $78, and COOKIE DECORATING KIT (KCD001), $48, from Martha By Mail, 800-950-7130. NINETEENTH-CENTURY BLOWN-GLASS JAR, $1,200, from Nancy Boyd Antiques, 2466 Main Street, P.O. Box 866, Bridgehampton, NY 11932; 516-537-3838.

page 79

LEAF-SHAPED GUM-PASTE CUTTERS from New York Cake & Baking Distributors, see above.

page 80

RED RIBBON from Hyman Hendler & Sons, see above. LEAF-SHAPED GUM-PASTE CUTTERS from New York Cake & Baking Distributors, see above.

page 81

GIANT REINDEER AND SNOW CRYSTAL COOKIE CUTTER SET (KMB008), $45, from Martha By Mail, 800-950-7130.

page 82

SILPAT BAKING MATS, $18 for 11¼" by 16½" (KSP002), $27 for 16½" by 24¼" (KSP001), from Martha By Mail, 800-950-7130.

GLITTER & GILDING

page 86

SILVER METALLIC ORGANZA, $14.95 per yard, from B&J Fabrics, 263 West 40th Street, New York, NY 10018; 212-354-8150. LOUIS XVI-STYLE CHAIRS from Pierre Deux Antiques, 369 Bleecker Street, New York, NY 10014; 212-243-7740. ⅞" TAPERS, $3.50 per pair for 18", $5 per pair for 24", from The Candle Shop, 118 Christopher Street, New York, NY 10014; 212-989-0148 or 888-823-4823. VICTORIAN GLASS GOBLETS from James II Galleries, Ltd., 11 East 57th Street, 4th Floor, New York, NY 10022; 212-355-7040. SILVER-PLATED SPHERE CARD HOLDERS (WPC001), $48 for set of six, from Martha By Mail; 800-950-7130.

page 87

GLITTER, Jimmy Jem's Powderz, $1.88 per tube, from Pearl Paint, 308 Canal Street, New York, NY 10013; 212-431-7932.

page 88

ANTIQUE SILVER RIBBON, $5 to $25 per yard, from Tinsel Trading Co., 47 West 38th Street, New York, NY 10018; 212-730-1030. GLITTER, Jimmy Jem's Powderz, $1.88 per tube, from Pearl Paint, see above. PINECONES from Winter Woods, 701 Winter Woods Drive, Glidden, WI 54527; 800-541-4511. Wholesale only; minimum order $250.

page 90

SPRAY PAINT, Krylon Original Chrome, $3.45 per can, from Pearl Paint, see above.

page 91 (and detail, page 136)

FEATHER CHRISTMAS TREE and METAL PROJECTS KIT (CMP001), $58, from Martha By Mail, 800-950-7130. ASSORTED ORNAMENTS from Matt McGhee, 22 Christopher Street, New York, NY 10014; 212-741-3138. ANTIQUE ORNAMENTS from Antique Articles, P.O. Box 72, North Billerica, MA 01862; 978-663-8083.

page 92

SILVER RIBBON from Bell'occhio, 8 Brady Street, San Francisco, CA 94103; 415-864-4048.

page 93

PHOTOGRAPHS by Victor Schrager. FRAMES from Bark Frameworks, 85 Grand Street, New York, NY 10013; 212-431-9080.

page 94

VENETIAN-GLASS VASE, $180, from DeVera, 384 Hayes Street, San Francisco, CA 94102; 415-861-8480. DRIED HOLLY from Dry Nature Designs, 129 West 28th Street, New York, NY 10001; 212-695-4104. PHOTOGRAPH by John Dugdale, represented by Wessel + O'Connor, 242 West 26th Street, New York, NY 10001; 212-242-8811.

page 95

HANDBLOWN AUSTRIAN GLASS BALL ORNAMENTS (CEG004), $24 for set of six, from Martha By Mail, 800-950-7130. ONION-SHAPED GLASS ORNAMENTS from Matt McGhee, see above.

page 96

ANTIQUE FRENCH SALAD PLATE from Pierre Deux Antiques, 369 Bleecker Street, New York, NY 10014; 212-243-7740. OCTAGONAL DRINKING GLASS from Gardner & Barr, 213 East 60th Street, New York, NY 10022; 212-752-0555.

page 97

SILVER-MESH RIBBON, $5 to $25 per yard, from Tinsel Trading Co., see above. PALE-GREEN TAFFETA RIBBON, $39.95 per yard for silk, $12.50 per yard for rayon, from Hyman Hendler & Sons, 67 West 38th Street, New York, NY 10018; 212-840-8393. Minimum order $75. EUCALYPTUS, SEEDED EUCALYPTUS, ACACIA BAILEYANA, AND SANTOLINA GARLAND from Green Valley Growers, 10450 Cherry Ridge Road, Sebastopol, CA 95472; 707-823-5583.

page 98

FRAMED FERN PRINTS, $480 each, from Reymer-Jourdan Antiques, 29 East 10th Street, New York, NY 10003; 212-674-4470. PAIR OF CIRCA 1820 SWEDISH PAINTED DEMILUNE TABLES, $3,800, from Evergreen Antiques, 1249 Third Avenue, New York, NY 10021; 212-744-5664. RUG from ABC Carpet & Home, 888 Broadway, New York, NY 10003; 212-473-3000. MOON AND STAR COOKIE CUTTER SET (KMB001), $45, NOAH'S ARK COOKIE CUTTER SET (CNA001) with nine copper animal cutters and template for ark, $78, and ENAMELWARE BUCKET (GWB001), 11" x 11½", $19, from Martha By Mail, 800-950-7130.

page 100

STYROFOAM CONE and FAUX FRUIT from Kervar, Inc., 119 West 28th Street, New York, NY 10001; 212-564-2525. SILVER LEAF, $6.50 for book of 25, ALUMINUM LEAF, $3 for book of 25, COLORED LEAF, $32 for book of 20, WUNDA SIZE, and RONAN ACRYLIC CLEAR OVERCOAT from Baggot Leaf Co., 430 Broome Street, 2nd Floor, New York, NY 10013; 212-431-4653. BONDEX QUICK PLUG available at hardware stores nationwide.

page 101

CIRCA 1880 FRENCH SILVER FOOTED BOWL, $2,825, from Nancy Corzine, 979 Third Avenue, New York, NY 10022; 212-223-8340. SMALL SILVER-PLATED FOOTED BOWL from Sentimento, 306 East 61st Street, New York, NY 10021; 212-750-3111. ARTIFICIAL FRUIT from Kervar, Inc., see above. CUSTOM LEAFING ON FRUIT by Franco

Eliali, 909 40th Street, No. 2, Brooklyn, NY 11219; 718-871-1167. ANTIQUE SILVER RIBBON, $5 to $25 per yard, from Tinsel Trading Co., see above. SILVER PAPER LEAVES, $5 for package of 25, from D. Blümchen & Company, P.O. Box 1210M, Ridgewood, NJ 07451; 201-652-5595.

FRUIT ARRANGEMENTS

page 102

GOLD-MESH LEAVES, $24 per dozen, from Dulken & Derrick, 12 West 21st Street, New York, NY 10010; 212-929-3614.

page 103

CIRCA 1800 GERMAN MAHOGANY CHAIRS WITH LEATHER SEATS, $12,500 for set of six, from Evergreen Antiques, 1249 Third Avenue, New York, NY 10021; 212-744-5664. ROUND TABLE from ABC Carpet & Home, 888 Broadway, New York, NY 10003; 212-473-3000. GLASSES from William Yeoward Crystal, 41 Madison Avenue, New York, NY 10010; 800-818-8484. Catalog available. ANTIQUE DECANTER, about $250, Barbara Trujillo, Kinnaman & Ramaekers, Inc., and Nancy S. Boyd, all at 2466 Main Street, P.O. Box 866, Bridgehampton, NY 11932; 516-537-3838.

page 105

REGENCY NEO-GOTHIC SIDE CHAIRS, $16,000 for four, from Karl Kemp Antiques, 34 East 10th Street, New York, NY 10003; 212-254-1877. LOUIS XVI CONSOLE, $12,000, from Reymer-Jourdan Antiques, 29 East 10th Street, New York, NY 10003; 212-674-4470.

page 106

FRENCH FAUTEUIL UPHOLSTERED WITH ANTIQUE TOILE, $3,200, from Gomez Associates, 504 East 74th Street, 3rd Floor, New York, NY 10021; 212-288-6856. YELLOW JUNO VASE, $70 for 9" x 5"; $85 for 8" x 7", from Ad Hoc Softwares, 410 West Broadway, New York, NY 10012; 212-925-2652.

page 107

SILVER-PLATED URNS, $30 each, from VSF, Inc., 204 West 10th Street, New York, NY 10014; 212-206-7236. ANTIQUE SILVER RIBBON, $15 per yard, from Tinsel Trading Co., 47 West 38th Street, New York, NY 10018; 212-730-1030.

page 108

GOBLET from William Yeoward Crystal, see above.

page 109

CIRCA 1820 AUSTRIAN BIEDERMEIER CLOCK, $11,000, from Karl Kemp Antiques, 34 East 10th Street, New York, NY 10003; 212-254-1877. NINE-TEENTH-CENTURY SPANISH CRYSTAL CHANDELIER, $12,500 for pair, from Amy Perlin Antiques, 1020 Lexington Avenue, New York, NY 10021; 212-744-4923.

page 110

SPRAY MOUNT available at crafts stores nationwide. SILVER-TREE LEUCODENDRON from Fischer & Page, 134 West 28th Street, New York, NY 10001; 212-645-4106.

page 111

POLYSTYRENE CONE from Kervar, Inc., 119 West 28th Street, New York, NY 10001; 212-564-2525. GOBLETS from William Yeoward Crystal, see above.

page 112

VELVET IVY LEAVES WITH SPIRALS, $24 per dozen, from Dulken & Derrick, 12 West 21st Street, New York, NY 10010; 212-929-3614. SILVER SATIN RIBBON from Hyman Hendler & Sons, 67 West 38th Street, New York, NY 10018; 212-840-8393.

page 113

RIBBON from Hyman Hendler & Sons, see above.

pages 114 and 115

ANTIQUE PINK MURANO GLASS COMPOTE, $900, ANTIQUE MURANO GLASS WATER GOBLETS, $1,600 for eight, CHAMPAGNE GLASSES, $1,200 for eight, and ANTIQUE PINK MURANO GLASS

CANDLESTICKS, $900 for four, from Gardner & Barr, 213 East 60th Street, New York, NY 10022; 212-752-0555. TALL SILVER-PLATED CANDLESTICKS, $595 per pair, from Sentimento, 306 East 61st Street, New York, NY 10021; 212-750-3111. ANTIQUE VENETIAN MIRROR, $1,800, and CREAMWARE from John Rosselli, 523 East 73rd Street, New York, NY 10021; 212-772-2137. ANTIQUE FRENCH SILVER CANDLESTICKS, $3,970 per pair, from Nancy Corzine, 979 Third Avenue, New York, NY 10022; 212-223-8340. GUSTAVIAN-STYLE DINING CHAIRS, $1,250 to $1,500 per chair, from Pierre Deux Antiques, 369 Bleecker Street, New York, NY 10014; 212-243-7740. ANTIQUE ROMANIAN CARPET from ABC Carpet & Home, 888 Broadway, New York, NY 10003; 212-473-3000. MAHOGANY DINING TABLE WITH BRASS EDGING, $5,650, from Victor Antiques, 223 East 60th Street, New York, NY 10022; 212-752-4100.

SWEETS & COOKIES

page 116

DRIED HOLLY, $6.50 a bunch, from Dry Nature Designs, 129 West 28th Street, New York, NY 10001; 212-695-4104. GLITTER, Jimmy Jem's Powderz, $1.88 per tube, from Pearl Paint, 308 Canal Street, New York, NY 10013; 212-431-7932. ANTIQUE SILVER RIBBON, $5 to $25 per yard, from Tinsel Trading Co., 47 West 38th Street, New York, NY 10018; 212-730-1030. LATE-EIGHTEENTH-CENTURY OAK SIDE TABLE from Pierre Deux Antiques, 369 Bleecker Street, New York, NY 10014; 212-243-7740.

page 117

CIRCA 1800 LIVERPOOL POTTERY PLATE, $2,850 for set of ten, from James II Galleries, Ltd., 11 East 57th Street, 4th Floor, New York, NY 10022; 212-355-7040. RED LINEN FOR NAPKIN from B&J Fabrics, 263 West 40th Street, New York, NY 10018; 212 354 8150. 2" MOKUBA MESH RIBBON from M&J Trimming, 1008 Sixth Avenue, New York, NY 10018; 212-391-9072. GOLD JORDAN ALMONDS, $24 per pound, from Dean & DeLuca, 560 Broadway, New York, NY 10012; 212-431-1691 or 800-999-0306. Catalog $3.

page 119

HANDBLOWN GLASS COMPOTE, $170, from Barton Sharpe, Ltd., 66 Crosby Street, New York,

NY 10012; 212-925-9562. HANDMADE PAPER STARS from the Moravian Book Shop, 428 Main Street, Bethlehem, PA 18018; 610-866-5481 or 888-661-2888. SILVER RIBBON from M&J Trimming, 1008 Sixth Avenue, New York, NY 10018; 212-391-9072.

pages 120 and 121

SILPAT BAKING MATS, $18 for 11¼"-by-16½" mat (KSP002) and $27 for 16½"-by-24¼" mat (KSP001), from Martha By Mail, 800-950-7130. KEY-LIME CANDY CANES, 75¢ each, from Conch Tour Train Gift Shop, 501 Front Street, Key West, FL 33040; 305-292-8921. CANDY CANES by Asher Candy available at supermarkets nationwide.

page 122

ATECO COOKIE CUTTERS and GOLD DRAGÉES from New York Cake & Baking Distributors, 56 West 22nd, New York, NY 10010; 212-675-2253 or 800-942-2539.

page 123

PRESSED-GLASS CAKE STANDS, $37 for 8" plate (KGP003), $39 for 10" plate (KGP004), $42 for 12" plate (KGP005), or $99 for set of three (KGP006), from Martha By Mail, 800-950-7130. RED VICTORIAN ETCHED GLASSES, $192 for six, from L. Becker Flowers, 217 East 83rd Street, New York, NY 10028; 212-439-6001.

page 126

SILPAT BAKING MATS, $18 for 11¼"-by-16½" mat (KSP002) and $27 for 16½"-by-24¼" mat (KSP001), from Martha By Mail, 800-950-7130.

page 127

DARK-CHOCOLATE TWIGS, $5.95 per box, Saraments du Médoc, from Balducci's, 424 Sixth Avenue, New York, NY 10011; 800-225-3822. BLANCHED ALMOND FLOUR, $5.95 per 1-pound bag, from A. L. Bazzini, Co., 339 Greenwich Street, New York, NY 10013; 212-334-1280. EDIBLE SILVER LEAF from New York Cake & Baking Distributors, see above.

pages 128 and 129

CIRCA 1840 DECANTER, $1,750 for a pair, from James II Galleries, Ltd., 11 East 57th Street, 4th Floor, New York, NY 10022; 212-355-7040. GILT-WOOD MIRRORED SCONCE and EBONIZED-AND-GILT AMERICAN CHAIR from John Rosselli International, 523 East 73rd Street, New York, NY 10021; 212-772-2137. To the trade only.

INDEX

CONTRIBUTORS

Special thanks to Eric A. Pike, the design director of MARTHA STEWART LIVING, *and to the many photographers, editors, art directors, and stylists whose inspirational ideas contributed to the creation of this volume, notably Stephana Bottom, Esther Bridavsky, Claudia Bruno, Anthony Cochran, James Dunlinson, Stephen Earle, Agnethe Glatved, Malcolm Hill, Joelle Hoverson, Jocelyn Joson, Fritz Karch, Jodi Levine, Christopher Maya, Hannah Milman, Sara Neumeier, Ayesha Patel, Lynn Ringland, Scot Schy, Kevin Sharkey, Susan Spungen, Susan Sugarman, Gael Towey, Tina Townsend, Gregory Wegweiser, and Christina Wressel. And thanks to the entire staff of Martha Stewart Living Omnimedia and to everyone at Oxmoor House, Clarkson Potter, Satellite Graphics, and Quebecor Printing whose invaluable work helped produce this book.*

PHOTOGRAPHY

Bill Abranowicz
front and back covers, pages 2, 4, 7 (center), 9, 18, 33, 44–48, 50, 51, 53 (bottom), 54, 55 (top), 56 (top right), 59, 60, 62, 75, 86–88, 90–94, 96–99, 130, 131, 136, 137, 142

Anthony Amos
page 57

Christopher Baker
pages 7 (right), 70, 71, 76, 77 (right), 80, 81, 84–85, 101, 102, 105, 107, 112 (right), 113, 114 (left), 115, 125, 127, 132, 141

Carlton Davis
pages 58, 63–69

Stewart Ferebee
page 5

Dana Gallagher
pages 3, 6, 8, 31, 35, 37 (right), 39 (top), 95 (bottom), 103, 106, 108, 109, 110 (top right), 111 (bottom row), 112 (left), 114 (right), 139, 140

Thibault Jeanson
pages 24 (top row), 30, 34, 36, 37 (left), 38, 39 (middle row; bottom row), 40–43

Amy Neunsinger
pages 72, 83, 116, 117, 119, 123, 124, 126 (bottom row, right), 128–129, 135

Matthew Septimus
pages 24 (bottom row), 25, 52, 53 (top row), 55 (bottom row), 77 (left), 78, 79, 82, 95 (top row), 100, 110 (top left; bottom row), 120, 126 (top row; bottom row, left)

Simon Watson
pages 7 (left), 10–13, 15–17, 19, 20, 22, 23, 26–29, 56 (top left; bottom), 111 (top row; middle row), 121, 138

ILLUSTRATIONS

Harry Bates
pages 65, 66, 69

If you have enjoyed this book, please join us as a subscriber to MARTHA STEWART LIVING *magazine. The annual subscription rate is $26 for ten issues. Call toll-free 800-999-6518, or visit our Web site. www.marthastewart.com.*